Boxers & Bluejackets

DEFENDERS OF LEGATIONS

Boxers & Bluejackets

A Personal Account by a Midshipman of
the Royal Naval Brigade
During the Boxer Uprising, China 1900

Charles C. Dix

LEONAUR

Boxers & Bluejackets
*A Personal Account by a Midshipman of the Royal Naval Brigade During
the Boxer Uprising, China 1900*
by Charles C. Dix

First published under the title
The World's Navies in the Boxer Rebellion (China 1900)

Leonaur is an imprint
of Oakpast Ltd

Copyright in this form © 2016 Oakpast Ltd

ISBN: 978-1-78282-485-5(hardcover)
ISBN: 978-1-78282-486-2 (softcover)

http://www.leonaur.com

Publisher's Notes

Contents

DEDICATED

BY

KIND PERMISSION

TO

THE RIGHT HONOURABLE EARL SPENCER

K.O., P.C.

(LATE FIRST LORD OF THE ADMIRALTY)

IN GRATITUDE FOR HIS HAVING GIVEN ME A NOMINATION

FOR THE NAVY, AND FOR THE GENEROUS PATRONAGE

OF HIS LORDSHIP, AND HIS LATE FATHER, TO MY

GRANDFATHER AND GREAT-GRANDFATHER, WHO

HAD THE HONOUR MEDICALLY TO ATTEND

THE HOUSEHOLD AT ALTHORP PARK,

FOR NEARLY A CENTURY.

Preface

In placing this little book before the public I well know its many shortcomings. The notes from which it was compiled were made on the spot, and in the feverish excitement of the times. But the subsequent duties and examinations of a British midshipman left me very little time to devote to its completion. Hence the delay in publication, and the probability that some mistakes may have crept in. It has no claim to be historical, but rather to be interesting and anecdotal, being largely interspersed with incidents which occurred between June and October 1900. Names have been excluded as far as possible for the very best reasons, and an endeavour has been made throughout neither to overstate the mistakes and excesses of other nations, and our own share in the proceedings, nor to understate their gallantry and our own discrepancies.

The personal pronoun is, I know, objectionable. My excuse for using it as often as I do, is that one man has but one pair of eyes, and I plead some little interest on the occasions when I feel compelled to use it. I believe that chapters 1, 2, 5, 6, 7, 8, 9, 10, 11 (more or less) and 14 will be fairly free from errors, as I was present at the events which took place in them. For the other chapters I cannot personally vouch, but trouble has been taken in compiling them from either letters or narratives of eye-witnesses. I take this opportunity of thanking all my fellow-officers and others who have very kindly helped me in this way, or in the no less important illustrative work. The latter are mostly from photographs by officers with the brigade. In conclusion, I trust that in my endeavour to get interest into incident, I have not, however innocently, trodden on the corns of anyone associated with our brigade.

C. C. Dix.

CHAPTER 1

Prelude

I do not propose to do more than touch lightly on the causes which led up to the great Boxer outbreak in June 1900``, but some misapprehension may be removed, and the reader of this volume may be led to more easily understand the state of affairs which obtained immediately before hostilities broke out, if a short explanation be given.

One hears many different opinions as to the reason of the Boxer outbreak, which every one will admit was the most important *casus belli* between the European Powers and China, and which eventually plunged the north of China into a sanguinary war which was waged on both sides with great fierceness

The missionaries, the Dynasty, and the universal hatred of the "foreign debbel" have all come under notice as the possible causes of the trouble, but there is no room to doubt that the last is the real one, and in fact the only one at all supportable.

Everything seems to point to the fact that the empress had long since desired to see the back of the troublesome foreigner, and although she sent her troops for the apparent reason of putting down the Boxers, there can be no doubt that she saw in the new movement a splendid opportunity for "ousting" all Europeans, thereby gaining a new place in the affections of her people, and a new lease of life for the Manchu Dynasty.

If this supposition be correct, she played her hand with marvellous cunning.

Imperial troops were sent against the rebellious (?) people, and in the middle of the fight that ensued, half of them would change sides, while the other half would amuse themselves by firing heavily into the mob with blank cartridges.

One general indeed did attack and defeat the Boxers, but he was sent for to Pekin, and was lucky to only lose his rank.

A very common question is "who were the Boxers?" and the answer is almost invariably, "Oh, some society or other which was formed for the expulsion of foreigners."This may be all right as far as it goes, but they were more than that. At the beginning of June they were ninety *per cent* of the male population in the affected provinces, between the ages of fourteen and sixty. They were fanatics of an extraordinary type, and declared that by virtue of certain drills, which they assiduously practised, they were immune from harm at the hands of their enemies.

In this belief they were in no wise shaken by their first defeats, for they said that those who fell had not been sufficiently attentive to their ritual, and they exhorted each other to further efforts, lest a like fate should overtake others. It is only half right to say that they were formed for the expulsion of foreigners, for the movement was quite semi religious, and their doctrine violently anti-Christian in the first place,—*ergo*, anti-foreign in the second.

There is no doubt that considerable numbers of Chinese may be among the long roll of martyrs which China gave for the Christian faith, a short eighteen months ago; and doubtless their only half-human captors would serve up something quite devilishly exquisite by way of torture to those native converts who fell into their hands.

The headquarters of the society was in Shantung, but thanks to an enlightened and powerful Viceroy, in the person of Yuan-Shi-Kai, they had to move from his province, and so became the more numerous, and powerful in the neighbouring province of Chihli, in which is situated the capital.

They soon succeeded in completely terrorising all the inhabitants who did not join their standard of their own free will, or rather of the madness born of mob violence. Here let it be understood that no one is more addicted to secret societies, or less addicted to mob violence, than a Chinaman. This sounds anomalous, but is nevertheless true. But once let loose a Chinese mob on the object of their hatred, and they compare very favourably with an Abu Klea Dervish, that is to say, that it is necessary to have "Maxims" to stop them. Again, a Chinaman would much rather argue any contested point out to a finish, knowing his own ability to "save face"; but once let him get pig-headed or obstinate in an unobtrusive sort of way, and it is well to go for a poleaxe.

The over-running of Chihli province brings the time of year up to the end of May, and it was not till then that the ministers of the Powers realised what a formidable movement was on foot. As a matter of fact, the ministers met on the 28th of May to consider the necessity of taking steps for their own safety, also for the protection of all Europeans, Americans, Japanese, and native Christians who were then in Pekin.

The outlook was far from reassuring. Fengtai, a station on the Pekin-Tientsin line, in close proximity to the capital, was in flames, railway communications with Tientsin had ceased, and it was believed that Boxers were even then employed in tearing up the rails.

The ministers decided to inform the Tsung-li-Yamen that they were asking their respective naval and military chiefs for Legation guards, and to beg them to afford the means of transport. The Tsung-li-Yamen, as usual, attempted to gain time by lies and procrastination; but in view of the uncompromising attitude of the British minister, they gave their grudging assent on the morning of the 31st May.

On the 29th May the general feeling of suspense was somewhat alleviated by the discovery that the line itself had not yet been damaged, and a train arrived from Tientsin with some officials who insisted on the resumption of traffic.

However, the attitude of the populace did not become any more friendly, and the soldiers who had been looked upon as possible protectors, now showed their true colours, by their bombastic and menacing demeanour. At length some Europeans were stoned, and threatened with weapons in broad daylight in the streets; and it was with feelings of relief that the foreign residents welcomed the guards, who to the number of 337, with several machine guns, arrived at the station at about 7 p.m. on May 31st.

Their arrival had an immediate effect, and for a day or two the situation became tolerably bearable.

Unfortunately their presence only intimidated the rowdies of Pekin and its nearest suburbs, and people kept flocking into the Legations from outlying districts, each with some tale more pitiable than the last.

On the 2nd of June news came of the desperate flight of the thirty-three Europeans from Pao-ting-fu, which resulted in the safe arrival of twenty-six of their number at Tientsin, and the still more desperate plight of Mr Norman, who, after the murder of his fellow missionary at Yung-Ching, had been taken prisoner to a village hard by, there to be dealt with by perhaps the most fiendishly cruel people on earth. Everything that was possible under the circumstances was done to save the unfortunate Englishman, but we know that protests were of no avail, and that he was done to death in a manner only to be conjectured. On the 4th June the storm broke, and railway communication was again interrupted,—more stations were burnt, and the whole countryside was ablaze.

Another meeting was convened, and after the Russian Minister had explained that a party of Cossacks, which had been allowed to go out to meet the Pao-ting-fu refugees, had been repulsed, and compelled to retreat to Tientsin without meeting the fugitives, the step was taken which gave the name to this volume. The ministers decided to telegraph instructions to their several admirals, and inform them what turn they thought the present crisis would assume, and also to ask them to take the necessary steps for the relief of the Europeans should all communication be stopped.

On the 5th June Sir Claude Macdonald had an extraordinary interview with the Tsung-li-Yamen, and during the conversation one of the illustrious body fell asleep, while the Legation interpreter was explaining something to the minister. Nothing was to be got from such men as these, who, even though they were headed by no less a person than Prince Ching, were at this juncture unable to make headway against the mob, and who, in fact, no longer voiced public opinion. Contradictory rumours emanating from the summer palace, where the empress was, concerning the whole question, were freely circulated, and the empress herself sent General Nieh against the Boxers, and followed up her order with another one, telling him that on no account was he to allow the Imperial troops to fire on them. A member of the useless Tsung-li-Yamen went so far as to taunt the minister by saying that he expected all the army would be Boxers in a day or two. In view of what occurred so soon afterwards, it was a significant statement to make.

It was eventually decided to petition the Throne, but after considerable discussion, it was resolved to wait until the 9th of June, as it was deemed inadvisable to demand an audience until the ministers had received the necessary authority from the home governments, to insist upon compliance. On the 8th June there was no change for the better in the situation, and Sir Claude telegraphed to Admiral Seymour to ask him for a further detachment of seventy-five men. It was on this day that definite news was received that General Nieh had withdrawn his troops to Lu-Tai, where there were immense stores of rice, and that the Boxers, finding themselves unopposed, had reached Yangtsun, an important walled town on the river, about 30 miles from Tientsin. Here they burnt the bridges, and began to tear up the rails, and it was finally realised that all hope of further communication with Tientsin was delayed for weeks. On this same day a massacre of native Christians took place at Tung-Chow, and some students were attacked out by the race-course.

In consequence of these acts, and sundry trustworthy rumours that Tung-fu-Hsiang, the general commanding the Kansu troops then in the district, had given out in public that he was only waiting for orders from his superiors—meaning the empress,—on receipt of which he would proceed to treat the foreigners in the same fashion as he had treated the unfortunate Mohammedans some four years previously, the ministers immediately telegraphed to the admiral, and informed him that the situation was extremely critical, and that unless reinforcements immediately advanced on Pekin, it was within the bounds of probability they might arrive too late to save the Europeans.

Even at this stage, the foreign ministers strove to put off the inevitable, and at a meeting that afternoon the majority of them supported the view that all available news pointed to a more favourable issue than Sir Claude Macdonald had been led at first to suppose. They agreed, however, to telegraph to their respective admirals at 2 o'clock on the following afternoon, if no signs were forthcoming that the ferment was subsiding.

Sir Claude, on his part, telegraphed to Sir Edward Seymour to inform him of the decision of his colleagues; but so certain was he about the turn of events, that he sent another telegram at 8 p.m. to Mr Charles, the British consul at Tientsin, which informed him of the deadly peril of the situation, and begging him to urge the senior naval officer to make all arrangements for an immediate advance on Pekin.

That evening, the 9th, all the outlying mission stations were handed over to the Chinese Government for safe keeping, till the troubles were over; the British Legation again became a place of refuge for many Europeans, and all possible means were utilised to put the place in a state of defence. While this drama, with, as it turned out, such a tragic sequel, was being enacted within the capital, a no less interesting one was taking place at Taku. As early as May the 30th, ships representing nearly every nation were collecting at the seaward gate of the capital.

The British representatives were the *Orlando* and the *Algerine*, and a hundred marines were landed from the two ships by four o'clock in the afternoon. At half-past nine that night eighty more men were dispatched to Tientsin by river, a distance of some sixty odd miles, in answer to a telegram which demanded further reinforcements. By this time Tientsin was trembling with suppressed excitement, and a most enthusiastic scene took place on the occasion of the already mentioned Pekin guards' departure. The next three days passed comparatively quietly, but a feeling of unrest pervaded the atmosphere, and some incendiaries attempted the destruction of the Chartered Bank. The attempt was foiled.

On the 1st June the unfortunates who were endeavouring to escape from Pao-ting-fu were heard of for the first time, and there was no lack of volunteers to seek them and bring them back. Besides the twenty-five Cossacks, two search parties, composed of civilians, were formed and succeeded in bringing them in on the 2nd. Safe the majority of them certainly were for the present, but their condition was pitiable, and the affair was not altogether satisfactory, as it was found that the reverse sustained by the Cossacks would act as a further incentive to all the rowdies in the neighbourhood.

On the 3rd, Admiral Seymour inspected the guards at Tientsin; and, being aware of the necessity of preparedness, he sent up a field gun and caused considerable numbers of bluejackets and marines to hold themselves in readiness for service. Outside the bar was gathered a huge fleet, and as each ship arrived, so did the guards in Tientsin increase in numbers.

On the 4th the native servants and others began to leave the settlement, and several of them besought their masters to go while there was yet time. "For," they assured them, "the foreigners are to be utterly exterminated on the 19th," which was, it will be remembered, the date of the last massacre of Tientsin in 1870.

In spite of these gloomy assurances, no general exodus took place from the settlement, and civilians, many of whom held posts under the government, and whose opinions were listened to with respect, were among the most positive that there would be no general rising. Even the most pessimistic clung to the hope that the Imperial army would protect them, if ever matters came to a head.

On the 6th an adventurous party determined to reconnoitre the line in the direction of Pekin, and managed to reach Yangtsun without hindrance. Here the train was boarded by General Nieh, who, it will be remembered, had been sent to deal with the Boxers armed with all sorts of contradictory orders.

The train proceeded for another fifteen miles, until, on reaching Lo-fa, bodies of Boxers were descried vigorously hacking down the telegraph poles, whilst others were burning sleepers and other railway material, in a similar energetic manner. This was enough for the cautious old Chinaman, and he politely but firmly refused to go further. His manner on the return journey betokened great alarm, and it was evident that he quite believed, in common with the majority of Chinese, that the Boxers were invulnerable. Be this as it may, an extraordinary rumour reached Tientsin on the following day, to the effect that he had engaged and defeated the Boxers with a loss of four hundred killed. An air of truth was given to this theory by the statement that he had been censured for his act, and had retired on Lu-Tai, where he was sulking with his army.

This last is probably entirely untrue, for no traces of any engagement were to be seen when the British commander-in-chief arrived on the scene a few days afterwards, except three harmless villagers, who were probably shot, not because they belonged to the rebellious faction, but for the opposite reason. Hundreds of bullets, with the appearance of being newly extracted from their cartridge cases, were found buried by the fires where Nieh's men had evidently encamped; and on the whole there are no grounds for hoping that he taught his, at that time supposed, opponents, such a salutary lesson as had been stated.

The next day another train left for the same purpose as the last, and it was found that during the night the Boxers had rendered it impossible to advance beyond Yangtsun without large repairs. However, it was surmised that the track was safe up to Yangtsun, and that a way might be forced along the line to Pekin by a sufficiently large force with the necessary repairing tools.

In consequence of this report it was decided by the various senior naval officers, at a conference on board the *Centurion*, that it was no use waiting until matters got worse, and that the Powers would therefore land brigades early next morning, and that the whole force under Sir Edward Seymour would try to push their way through to the aid of the beleaguered Legations. Amidst immense enthusiasm the sailors got ready for service, and the tugs belonging to the 'Taku Tug and Lighter Company' having been requisitioned, the force was landed at an early hour on the morning of the 10th. They left Tientsin on the

Taking the admiral to the final conference on
H.M.S. "Centurion"

same mornings and during the day more reinforcements were poured into the settlements from the now almost denuded fleet. On this date also fifty bluejackets were sent to Tongshan to protect the important railway works at that place. The work of the Naval Brigade was beginning.

On the 11th, trade in the settlement practically ceased; once busy thoroughfares were now desolate, and a sort of hushed expectancy took the place of the usual busy stir in the town. Armed men, however, were at this time of more importance than any number of Chinese hawkers, and a valuable addition to the powers of resistance arrived in the person of Commander Beatty, D.S.O. and a hundred and fifty men, shortly followed by two "Maxims." The day was spent in drawing up a more elaborate system of defence than had been thought necessary before, and an attempt was made to overawe the natives by a march round the suburbs.

In the afternoon there occurred the first piece of official interference on the part of the viceroy, who refused to allow a train to proceed up the line, which was packed with German troops. Now the Germans, when on active service, don't understand this sort of treatment, and the disorderly mob which, as is usual on these occasions, quickly gathered, was swept out of the way by the display of fixed bayonets, backed by the evident intention of using them if needs be. On this display of force, the viceroy no longer withheld his permission for the train to proceed, and the Germans reached their destination without further molestation. From this date communication practically ceased with the fleet, but 1770 Russians just managed to arrive in the nick of time, before ingress was finally barred.

Naturally the landing of a brigade, and the supplies necessary for its maintenance, entailed a large amount of work on the sadly depleted crews of the fleet outside the bar; but nobody was idle, and the work of equipping a further force was steadily proceeded with. Orders for stores, ammunition, men, and even cruisers followed one another with astonishing rapidity, and it was decided to telegraph to the general commanding troops at Hong-Kong to hold part of the garrison in readiness for immediate shipment to the troubled province. Meanwhile the Chinese were by no means idle; large stores of rice and munitions of war were daily poured into the strong forts at the mouth of the river. As a further step, they proceeded to mine its mouth, and it became apparent that they intended to block the only means of communication with the interior, and with the soon-to-be-allied gunboats, which were already anchored some distance up the waterway.

On the 15th a tug was dispatched in charge of a midshipman about thirty miles down the coast, to rescue some missionaries who were reported to be in distress; and in the evening the expectant fleets heard that Sir Edward Seymour had been in touch with the Boxers.

The Naval Brigade's work had commenced!

Conferences had been a matter of daily occurrence for some time, and on the morning of the 16th, on board the Russian flagship, at a conference which proved to be the most momentous of all, the Admirals agreed that the situation was such as to demand immediate action, which should take the form of an allied occupation of the Taku Forts. Accordingly an ultimatum was sent to the general in command, to the effect that if they were not evacuated by midnight 16th June, the allied forces would bombard and storm them.

During the morning the tug returned, the officer having successfully performed his task, and having reached his destination just in time to baulk the Boxers, who were in pursuit, of their prey.

Such, then, was the situation at noon on June the 16th, and it may be doubted whether any host of peasants, for whatever reason, had ever raised such a hornets' nest about their ears before.

Let it be remarked before dosing this prelude that the date was ill chosen. Those in the plot had meant that matters should reach a climax in the middle of November, when the river would have been frozen, and all hopes of sending aid futile. Their scheme failed for two main reasons. One was the drought which threatened starvation to thousands of the poorer classes, and which was, as a matter of course, laid at the door of the hated foreigner; the other was that not only the ringleaders of the movement, but even the government themselves, had lost all control over the minds and bodies of the fanatical Boxers, whose placards, which contained a great deal about "killing foreigners," were now posted up broadcast in every village.

CHAPTER 2

The Bombardment and Storming of the Taku Forts

The Taku Forts are four in number, two being situated on each side of the mouth of the Pei-Ho River. To seaward of them stretch large expanses of treacherous mud, just covered by the sea at high water; stakes have been driven into the slime for several hundred yards from the bottom of the embankments, and landing is quite impracticable at any state of the tide. On the landward side stretches a large plain, intersected with small canals and irrigation works, and immediately to the rear of the forts are the villages of Tong-Ku and Ta-Ku respectively. The only other things to attract attention are the small naval yard at Taku, and the pilot village at the mouth of the river, which has been built on the right bank.

Tong-Ku is about 3 miles up the river, and here are the railway station, coal stores, and the necessary landing stages for lading or unlading the merchant steamers which in some cases ply as far as Tientsin. The forts are protected against men-of-war, of a size larger than gunboats, by the bar, which is eleven and a half miles to seaward, and on which the depth of water varies from two feet to seventeen feet, at different states of the wind and tide. The trade of the place, which is important, has to be taken from Tong-Ku out to the ships lying about fourteen miles away, and this is done by the fleet of tugs and lighters belonging to the 'Taku Tug and Lighter Company,' which at present enjoys the monopoly.

This company and the railway are both British concerns, and before the outbreak, were both in a flourishing condition.

The forts themselves, the N., N.W., S., and New forts—the first two on the right bank and the others on the left bank,—were immensely powerful. Strong as they were in 1860, modern ordnance had made them practically impregnable; and to the ordinary observer it seemed that any attempt to forcibly occupy them would involve enormous losses of ships and men, and might end in disaster.

Had the defence of these positions been entrusted to any but Chinese, the lives and property of Europeans in the whole of Northern China would at this date have been of no account. The walls and parapets were constructed of mud mixed with chopped straw, a mixture which seems impervious to shell fire; they were constructed by a German syndicate, and a covered road connected the N.W. and N. forts. The armament was composed of guns of all sorts, sizes, and dates, but with heavy, modern, quick-firing guns the Chinese were extremely well supplied, and although the ancient armament did but little damage, it interfered in no way with the general impregnability of the positions.

At the naval yard were four new German-built destroyers with an estimated speed of thirty-five knots; they mounted six 3-pr. Q.F. guns each, and were capable of doing great damage if handled by officers with any self-reliance or ability; there was also a gunboat in dock, but she was probably denuded of her crew, and took no part in the subsequent proceedings.

From this it will be seen that the forts and the destroyers together comprised a formidable force against which the Allies could only pit the following:—

H.M.S. *Algerine*, a three-masted sloop, mounting six 4-in. Q.F. guns and several smaller Q.F. and machine guns, totally unprotected against gun fire, except her guns, which were fitted with shields. She has a speed of about thirteen and a half knots.

H.M.S. *Fame* and *Whiting*, two destroyers, each mounting one 12-pr. Q.F. and five 6-pr. Q.F., with a thirty knot speed.

The *Iltis* (German), with six 4.1-in. Q.F. guns, several pom-poms and other smaller Q.F. guns; also unarmoured, and very similar to the *Algerine*, but with a higher freeboard and slightly higher speed.

H.I.R.M.S. *Gilyak* (Russian), a new gunboat: one 4.7-in. Q.F., and six 12-pr. Q.F.—a pretty little ship which impressed the observer with a power she was far from possessing.

H.I.R.M.S. *Bobre* (Russian), an old steel gunboat, heavily built and clumsy to look at, mounting one 9-in. B.L., one 6-in. B.L., and several machine guns.

H.I.R.M.S. *Koreetz* (Russian) a similar vessel to the last, but with the heavier armament of two 8-in. B.L., one 6-in. B.L., and one or two other guns of no importance. This ship had the heaviest, though probably the least efficient armament of any of the allied squadron yet mentioned.

Lion (French), an ancient old gunboat mounting two 5.5-in. B.L. and a few very old-pattern machine guns.

H.I.J.M.S. *Atago* (Japanese), an old iron gunboat mounting one 8.2 M.L. and one 4.7, with a few obsolete machine guns.

U.S.S. *Monocacy* (American), an entirely obsolete wooden paddle-wheel steamer, with only M.L, smooth-bore guns for her main armament, and but three or four "Colt" machine guns. From this force must be deducted the useless *Monocacy* for the above very good reasons, and the *Atago*, which was full of explosives, and landed the majority of her crew for the storming party.

Thus the Allies had only five *unprotected* gunboats, mounting a fairly heavy armament, it is true, but of necessity so disposed that, as a rule, not half the guns would bear on the enemy at once. Another and more serious handicap was the extreme narrowness of the river, about two hundred yards, and the impossibility of escape should the attack fail

Immediately the decision of the admirals had been made known, all became bustle and activity on the ships outside the bar. Officers and men vied with one another in the work of getting everything ready to equip the storming party, and every one was strapping up blankets, filling water-bottles, buckling on bandoliers, cutlasses, revolvers, and all the other man-killing paraphernalia which sailor and soldier alike carry. All hands were happy, except the unfortunate few who, for various reasons, were unable to go, and not even the ceremony of being presented with a field-service dressing by the doctor, brought a thoughtful face to the eager men.

Of rough, rude jests there were plenty. A brawny bluejacket looked at the small package containing gauze, lint, and bandage, and asked, "'Ere, Bill, what's this for?"

"Why, to tie up the Chinamen, of course."

"Well, this won't be big enough when I've finished with 'em; give me another dozen."

And so it went on until the "fall in" sounded, and the various ships' detachments fell in on the "*Barfleur's* quarter-deck to receive the good wishes of the unlucky minority, and a few words of sound advice

H.M.S. "Centurion"—Marines getting ready to land.

from the Rear Admiral. At precisely 3.25 p.m. the tug *Fa-Wan* left the *Barfleur*, flying the white ensign, with three hundred and twenty officers and men on board, or in the boats towing astern. On the way ashore the men were told off into separate companies; the commander formed his staff; and then, for the first time, men began to realise what was in front of them; and so, when the forts came into view, they came in for a good deal of attention.

Whatever the men thought, only one sentiment was expressed:

"The admiral is in danger, our shipmates are in danger, and as a small beginning to relieve them we're going to take those forts."

No doubt it was generally felt that the force was comparatively puny; but, for cogent and self-evident reasons, the Indian Army was yet thousands of miles away, and after all it was right that the commander-in-chief should be relieved by the navy; beside which there was a chance of avenging the repulse of some forty years back for the second time.

As soon as details on the forts became distinguishable to the naked eye, the Chinese gunners were seen to be standing to their guns, and a range-finder, which had been placed in position since noon that day, was manned by a crowd of laughing Chinese, whose sole cause for merriment appears to have been, as they thought, the entrance of the "foreign devils" into their well-laid trap. Their folly cost them dear!

The tug ran alongside the *Algerine*, and the work of trans-shipment was quickly over. Ammunition boxes were opened up, bandoliers and pouches filled, food was served out, and then men were billeted to sleep in different parts of the upper deck. By the time this work had been finished, the night had fallen, and half an hour afterwards the pipe went "Hands up anchor." The *Algerine* weighed, and moved a few hundred yards up the river to take her pre-concerted position.

This simple move no doubt had a great effect on the issue of the engagement, as far as the *Algerine* was concerned, for the Chinese had doubtless trained their guns on her when she was in her former position, and they must have known her range to a few yards. She was the van ship in the line, with the *Iltis*, *Gilyak*, *Koreetz*, *Bobre*, and *Lion* astern of her, in the order named. At this time, however, the *Iltis* and *Lion* had not taken up their positions; and as there was some chance of them being torpedoed by the four Chinese destroyers as they moved down the river, the captain of the *Algerine* directed the captains of our two destroyers to move up the river and seize them at 1.30 a.m.

As the pre-arranged hour for starting the bombardment was 2

a.m., and as there were few who felt sleepily inclined, the spare hours were given up to discussing whether the Chinese would accept the ultimatum and run, or whether the allies would find themselves engaged in a few hours' time. This was decided in a most abrupt manner, for at 12.50, or one hour and ten minutes before the allies were going to start, a shell shrieked over the *Algerine* in unpleasant proximity to her topmasts. This was followed by an almost simultaneous fire from every gun that would bear on the little squadron. In the midst of this storm the most perfect discipline prevailed on board the British ship. Quickly and quietly the storming party were got down into the boats ready alongside, the guns' crews closed up to their guns, and the *Algerine* fired the first shot of retaliation in an incredibly short space of time.

An incident worthy of mention occurred during the first hail of shell. A man on the *Algerine's* poop saw a figure climbing leisurely aloft; he hailed it with "Where are yer goin'? are yer goin' to do a bloomin' sleep in the cross-trees?"

"No, I ain't exac'ly tired just now; I'm doin' the correc' thing, though; I'm just goin' to nail the bloomin' colours where they can see 'em"

This very naturally created a laugh. Other jokes were cracked, and half deaf, men worked their guns for six hours with a fixed grin on their countenances, born half of amusement, half of the indefinable something which steals over men on coming face to face with death for the first time.

For the first hour of the bombardment the storming party were lying alongside the *Algerine* in boats, and immediately before landing, which took place without mishap at 2.30 a.m., a ration of hot cocoa was served oat to each man.

Much happened in this first hour; at one o'clock, or ten minutes after the commencement of the engagement, the *Gilyak* turned on her searchlight, and very naturally she became the object of the undivided attention of the enemy's gunners. Three shells struck her almost immediately; a steam pipe was severed, a magazine exploded, and the third projectile entered her bows on the waterline. Her fore compartment filled, and if the depth of water had been greater there is good reason to suppose that she would have foundered; as it was, her searchlight was extinguished, and she became nearly incapable of further action.

A neat piece of work, encompassing the capture of the hostile destroyers, had also taken place. As soon as the forts commenced firing, the *Whiting* and *Fame* weighed, and proceeded up river at a distance apart of three hundred yards, this being the distance between the second and fourth destroyers. Each towed a whaler manned by a boarding party of twelve men and one officer. The idea was to pass well out in the stream, to give the enemy the idea that our boats were only intent on proceeding up river, and when the *Fame's* bow should be abreast of number four, and the *Whiting's* of number two, to sheer in and board them, each whaler boarding number three and number one respectively. This was effected most successfully.

After a trifling resistance and the exchange of a few shots the crews were driven overboard or below hatches, with the loss of a few killed and wounded. Our casualties were nil, and beyond a slight twist to the *Fame's* bow, neither the prizes nor our destroyers suffered any injury. The enemy were ready, and yet displayed an entire lack of resource and pluck. Their ammunition was on deck, and torpedoes, minus their warheads, in the tubes; and it is difficult to estimate the damage that they might have inflicted had they been in the hands of men of action instead of nerveless cowards.

Immediately after their capture the *Iltis* and *Lion* moved down river and took up their positions in the line of gunboats, and as there was a good deal of sniping at the prize crews from the naval yard, the four little ships slipped their cables and were towed up beyond Tong-Ku. On their way they had to pass a mud battery, which fired at them without fear of a reply, as it lay between our destroyers and the Russian gunboats. It was here that the *Whiting* was struck, and it was at first supposed that the little battery had been the cause of the trouble, but it was afterwards found that the projectile which tore through her side, and lodged in one of her water-tube boilers, was a 5-in. shell, which makes it practically certain that it was fired from one of the forts. Luckily it did not burst, and beyond damaging several tubes and putting the boiler out of action, it caused no damage.

By 5 a.m. the four prizes were berthed securely at Tong-Ku, and the *Fame* and *Whiting's* share in the action ceased when they convoyed a tug, with despatches and stores for Tientsin, past a fort twelve miles up the river, the garrison of which looked threatening. It had been arranged that the storming party were not to make any forward movement until the heavy guns in the N.W. fort had been effectively silenced by the fire from the gunboats; so the whole force lay down somewhat in the order in which they were going to commence the

H.M.S. "Barfleur"—Bluejackets landing.

advance, and watched the duel with breathless interest. The actual land force engaged was 904 officers and men, and as it was proposed by the German and Japanese commanders that the British senior officer should direct the operations, the honour fell to Commander (now Captain) Cradock of H.M.S. *Alacrity*. The composition of the force was as follows:—

British—23 officers, 298 men; Japanese—4 officers, 240 men; German—3 officers, 130 men; Russian—2 officers, 157 men; Italian—1 officer, 24 men; Austrian—2 officers, 20 men; together making the above total.

The first advance commenced at about three o'clock in the morning; the distance being 1300 yards. The British, Japanese, and Italians (the latter having brigaded themselves with our men), were in the fighting line, with the Germans, Austrians, and Russians for supports and reserves. The plan of attack was to advance in extended order to within fifty yards of the moat on the north front, then swing to the right, charge along the military road between the river and moat on the west face, and endeavour to force an entrance at the west gate.

Once into the outer fort, it was expected that the enemy would either flee or surrender. If not, an entry into the inner fort was to be forced as opportunity offered. The advance continued until the fighting line reached a point about a thousand yards from the fort, when it became evident that the fort had suffered but slightly from gun fire, and that the majority of its guns were still intact. An attack under these conditions would have entailed serious losses, and it was decided to wait until daylight, more especially as the intervening ground was not well known.

Dawn broke about 4 a.m., and was heralded by a tremendous explosion in the South fort; a lucky shot had pierced a magazine, which blew up and wrought immense damage. As soon as it was light too, the firing from the *Algerine* became superb, and the firing from the other vessels gained considerably in accuracy. Shot after shot fell right on top of the guns in the N.W. fort; and although the Chinese gunners returned again and again to their work, and fought their guns most pluckily, it was impossible to stand before such a well-directed fire; and by 4.30 this fort was silenced.

A moment to reflect on the probable effects of a naval engagement, and the line of stormers advanced. Immediately the gunboats ceased their fire, and almost as immediately two Chinese field guns commenced shelling the advancing lines. But our chaps were tired of waiting, and had the fire been ten times as hot, nothing would have stopped them. Drill-book tactics fell to the ground. The force started at a steady double, halted at 800 yards, and fired two volleys; the same at 500 yards; once more at 300 yards; then 'the charge' was sounded! The order "supports into the fighting line"; "fix bayonets"; and away we all dashed, gradually converging on the N.W. corner of the fort. The area over which the attack passed was hard mud, quite flat and without a vestige of cover.

At about 200 yards from the moat, however, there was an extensive stretch of impassable ground, and this necessitated a certain amount of crowding in order to reach the road which ran along the river bank. It was here that most of the casualties occurred, but without a check the British and Japanese fixed bayonets, gave several cheers, and went at them bald-headed, rushing the west gate, and soon finding themselves in possession of the outer fort. Some little delay, just sufficient to allow the majority of the enemy to escape pell-mell in the direction of Peh-tang,. took place here; and it was some minutes before the inner fort was gained.

As we went in they went out, and nearly all opposition ceased. There was a race for the two flag-staffs: the Chinese Yellow Dragons were torn down, and amidst an outburst of cheering the White Ensign was hoisted, closely followed by the Red Sun of Japan. I used my pistol for the first time here. My lieutenant and myself were standing in the square cheering our flag going up, with our men taking cover in a passage, when two Chinese nipped out of a gateway about twenty yards away, and came for us with fixed bayonets, firing their magazines as they marched, from the hip. My lieutenant had emptied his revolver and was drawing his sword to defend himself when I chipped in and "bagged the brace."

No sooner did the enemy in the South and North forts recognise the fall of the inner fort, than they turned several guns on to the occupants, but the gunboats were by this time moving down the river, except the damaged *Gilyak*; and the British and Japanese sailors retaliated with two captured guns, gradually causing the Chinese fire to diminish.

There was no time to be wasted, and in a quarter of an hour the force was on the move again, marching along the covered way between the N.W. and N. forts.

While still a quarter of a mile from the N. fort a deafening explosion, followed by an immense column of dust and smoke, was heard and felt in the direction of the *Iltis*. So great was the shock, that it was distinctly heard, and the effects clearly visible to the fleet fourteen miles away. A shell from the *Algerine* had exploded a 6-inch gun magazine, and for some time the air was so thick with dust that the men belonging to the landing party could scarcely see. They, however, jumped on to the mud parapet, and commenced to cheer the gunboats, but were driven down again by a shell which landed just below them. The moral effect of a disaster like this must be tremendous, but the gunners redoubled their fire, and two minutes later the *Iltis* got badly 'hulled' several times, and lost heavily. The *Algerine*, owing to her by this time almost point-blank range, only got struck in her cowls and upper works, and her loss in men was comparatively small.

From that moment the Chinese in the North fort lost heart, and no resistance was offered; so that in ten minutes' time the Germans entered by one gate, the British by the landward gun ports; and the allied flags were hoisted over the last fort on the left bank of the river.

An unexpected amount of opposition was offered by a single 6-inch Q.F. Armstrong in the South fort, but the captured guns in the last position, in conjunction with the gunboats, succeeded in silencing it after a desperate duel. The gun shield was found to have been struck seven times, and the cement emplacement was literally torn to pieces by shell fire. If the other guns had been served with the same devotion as this one, and those of the first fort to fall, the allies' losses must have been doubled at least.

Boats were procured without delay, immediately the shell fire ceased, and the British force crossed the river to attack the largest and most powerful of all the enemy's strongholds. Not a shot was fired! The two explosions referred to had caused terrific damage to the fort itself, and these, together with the heavy bombardment, had entirely unnerved the Chinamen, who fled precipitately as soon as the bluejackets effected a landing. The heavy guns mounted in the New fort luckily would not 'bear' during any part of the engagement, and these too surrendered without firing a shot.

By seven o'clock the storming party were back on board their respective ships to get some breakfast, before landing again to make good the terms of the ultimatum.

The engagement had lasted for six hours, and the Chinese had lost at least 650 men. The official despatch gives the Chinese loss in the N.W. and N. forts at 100, and quite 150 more must have perished in the explosions, and under the heavy shell fire to which the South fort was subjected. The allies' loss was altogether 172 officers and men, most of them being wounded. An hotel in the little pilot village, at the mouth of the river, was turned into a hospital, and here the British wounded received every attention possible under fairly favourable circumstances. The next thing to be done was the forming of garrisons for the forts, and the making of dispositions whereby the European force might follow up this, their first brilliant success.

CHAPTER 3

The First Siege of Tientsin

By the siege of Tientsin is meant the siege of the European settlements by the Chinese, not, as might be supposed, the siege of the native walled city by the allies; this latter event not taking place until the settlements had successfully withstood the attack of some 30,000 Chinamen for two successive periods, broken by the first relief, of altogether a calendar month.

The settlements are built on the right bank of the river, to the eastward of the native city, and abut on the Chinese suburbs. They and the native city alike are enclosed by the same mud wall, a structure about 12 feet high, and broad enough on the top for four men to walk abreast, called "Sankolinsin's folly." Four miles to the north-eastward of the British settlement was the large and important arsenal known as the Pei-Yang; a mile and a half to the south-westward was a smaller arsenal called Hi-Kuan-Su; and six and a half miles to the northward was the large and valuable military store, which went by the name of the Hsi-Ku arsenal. All these positions were already full of Imperial troops by the 15th of June, and as we know, the whole country was swarming with semi-religious fanatics.

On the night of the 15th a great part of the French settlement, which lay nearest to the city, was burnt by Boxers, and the troops spent the night under arms. A train with a searchlight, which had been cleverly fitted up at very short notice by an engineer from the British flagship, patrolled the line till daybreak, and 200 Russians were sent to a station situated half-way between Tientsin and Taku, with orders to keep the line open and prevent damage being done to the buildings. Inside the settlement the people were busy building barricades in the streets, loopholing walls, and placing staging for riflemen to stand on behind them.

NATIVE QUARTER, TIENTSIN, (FROM PONTOON BRIDGE), DESTROYED BECAUSE DANGEROUS TO EUROPEANS ON ACCOUNT OF HARBOURING CHINESE SOLDIERS.

On the night of the 16th an attack was made in force by the Boxers, who deliberately burnt the native suburbs lying between the city and the settlement, doing pounds' worth of damage to their own people in the futile attempt to burn out the foreigners. After a time they incautiously moved across the Russians' front, and immediately came under a steady fire, which, together with the fire of two guns, drove them over towards the British settlements. Here they were similarly dealt with by our sailors and marines; and about 5 a.m. they drew off, having suffered heavily.

On Sunday, the day that the Taku Forts fell, a repairing train, which had been sent out to clear the line, was fired upon by Imperial troops, whereupon an armoured train was despatched to the spot with 200 Russians, who put them to flight after losing a few men. At two o'clock on the same day the first shells came whizzing over the settlement, and it was generally recognised for the first time, by the commanding officers, that the existing state of affairs virtually meant war with China. The prospect was hardly brilliant; inside the settlement was a mixed force of 2400 men, with nine field guns, and a few machine guns; outside were 15,000 Imperial troops, with immense numbers of modern quick-firing guns. Their ammunition was of the best, and practically unlimited, and they had the dreaded Boxers at their back.

The perimeter to be defended was about five miles long, of which one-third was partially protected from a rush by the mud wall, as much more by the river, while on the third side, the Chinese houses were so close that it was practically indefensible. Ammunition was very limited in quantity, and the only thing from which encouragement could be drawn, was the fact of having several hundred women and children to defend against the execution of the hideous threats printed on the multifarious posters which had been sent to all the Chinese in the settlement, to induce them to leave before too late. A further source of weakness was the railway station, which was actually isolated on the opposite bank of the river, and which had to be held at all costs. This arduous task fell to the Russians by reason of their numbers. Much loss of life was undoubtedly saved by a very smart little engagement which took place as soon as shelling commenced.

Opposite the eastern end of the British portion of the bund stood some tin-roofed barracks. surrounded by a wall, where a number of embryo officers and some hundreds of Chinese troops had established themselves. With them were a battery of Krupp guns, and it was doubtless their intention to open fire on the settlement at point-blank range as soon as they got their orders from the authorities. Luckily those orders had not arrived at the time that the first gun was fired, and in the interval, their calculations were upset by an attack on the position by the British marines. The representatives of this fine corps, supported by some British and German bluejackets, crossed the river and stormed the building.

The Chinese, a great many of whom corresponded to our military cadets, called themselves the "Fight to the death Boys"; they acted right well up to their boast, for very few escaped! The effect was decisive, and in half an hour after a desperate hand-to-hand fight, the enemy fled, numbers being killed as they ran; the building was burnt and the guns captured. On this day the fifty bluejackets, who, with a lieutenant and two midshipmen, had been sent to guard Tongshan on the 10th, arrived at Pei-ta-ho. Their little expedition had not been devoid of interest. Tongshan is the seat of the most important railway works in the north of China; it is situated on the branch line to Shan-Hai-Kwan, and was right in the path of the rising. As its fall would involve enormous pecuniary loss to the company, a guard had been asked for, and the above-named force had left Tientsin with that purpose.

Their troubles commenced early, for at Lutai, a place half way between Tong-Ku and their destination, the train stopped for water. Had it not been for the order to avoid showing themselves as much as possible, it is probable that they would never have left the place alive, for there was a large force of Imperial troops at the station with orders to open fire should any European force attempt to detrain. This incident should suffice to show how the Chinese government kept faith with the foreigners, because at that time it was distinctly understood that the allied forces and the Imperial troops were working together for the suppression of a common nuisance. The bluejackets reached Tongshan that evening, where they received an enthusiastic welcome from the small community who seemed rather unnecessarily alarmed. However that may have been, they could not do enough for the officers and men, who found excellent accommodation and a good meal awaiting them.

At a first glance the situation seemed to be not especially dangerous, but the attitude of the Chinese troops in the vicinity put a different complexion on matters. Of these, there were 300 encamped half a mile away, whereas the Europeans numbered twenty-four, of whom twenty-three were men and one a woman; the men were rather nervous, and the lady very ill. The first step taken was to send the lady to

Pei-ta-ho by a special train. This very naturally raised an argument, but it was pointed out that the force had been sent to protect them, and if they chose to oppose the measures which the commanding officer thought necessary, well, the force would go away. Nothing more was said. The next thing done was to commandeer 50 mauser rifles and 30,000 rounds of ammunition, which were going up country to the Chinese. These were served out to the civilians, and orders were given that all hands were to sleep in the main compound at nights; positions were assigned to them, and the place was put into a state of defence.

During the next day the Chinese troops left, and the day was spent in building flanking towers round the wall, and in otherwise strengthening the position. Their main compound was in the shape of a stringed bow, and was surrounded by an 8 foot high wall; when loopholed and completed it would have been a hard nut to crack without artillery, but against guns, the defence would have undoubtedly broken down. During the third night a compound adjoining the main building caught fire, and in the middle of this excitement a man was seen galloping about on horseback. His horse was promptly shot and he was taken prisoner. His explanations, however, seemed to be *bona fide*; and he stated that he had come from a camp near by, to ascertain the cause of the conflagration, when he had been fired upon and his horse killed. He was remunerated and released. The fire gradually burnt itself out, and for the next few days there was neither alarm nor excitement.

One morning, however, the dull distant booming of heavy guns from the direction of Taku made it evident that something out of the ordinary was afoot; and when a European arrived by train from that direction, all hands eagerly awaited his news. It was none of the best; he reported that the allies were attacking the Taku forts, that a furious bombardment was proceeding, and that the allies at present appeared to be making but little impression on the forts. He also volunteered that three of the gunboats had been sunk—a thing that had only occurred in his imagination—that the forts at Peh-tang had shelled his train, and that troops had searched it at Lu-Tai, telling the Chinese driver and stokers that if they had found any European on board, they would have killed everyone with him. He had escaped by hiding in the coal box.

This was alarming enough, and steps were taken to flee to Pei-ta-ho, where the *Humber* was in readiness to take refugees on board. But worse was to come, for at 9.15 a telegram was received from the above mentioned town, saying that General Ma, with 5000 men and 18 guns, was on his way south, and might be expected at Tongshan at 10 a.m. Praying seemed about the only thing to have recourse to now; but to use a platitude—"God *helps those who help themselves"*—so it was determined to do all that lay in their power to prevent Ma and his troops from remaining at Tongshan. Steam was raised in an engine, and a train was prepared in an out-of-the-way siding, and held in readiness for an immediate start in either direction. Should all arguments fail, it was decided to take up a position at point-blank range alongside the arrival platform, where it would be possible to create enormous havoc amongst the crowded troops, who, placed in such a position, would in all probability lose their heads and flee.

However, the unexpected happened, and on two Chinese servants in the telegraph department telling the commanding officer news had just been sent that his presence was essential further south immediately, and moreover that if he stopped at Tongshan his firemen and drivers would desert, he promptly put guards on his engines and steamed gaily off. The last that was heard of him was that he was detraining five miles away, having no doubt come to the conclusion that he had been duped. In half an hour's time the Europeans were beyond his reach, for on his departure they immediately proceeded in the opposite direction.

It seems rather ungrateful and rude to recapitulate the idiosyncrasies of some of the civilians who were so very kind to our men, and who were so loyal to their commander; but the idea of runaways taking all their household gods with them in such a crisis has its funny side, and it required in some cases a good deal of argument to make them relinquish their pianos and chests of drawers to the tender mercies of the Chinese. Having cut both wires and rail in their rear, they headed for Pei-ta-ho, and their escape from an extremely dangerous and difficult position was brought to a successful issue at seven o'clock on the night of the 17th.

After this somewhat lengthy digression—which I trust will be excused as much on account of the fact that the events recorded took place at the same time as the opening days of the siege of Tientsin, as that they are interesting—we will return to Tientsin, which we left at a successful conclusion of the attack on the Military College. As may be imagined, the defenders and citizens of Tientsin were immensely elated at the result of their initial engagement, but on the morrow they were to be attacked instead of attacking, and to be attacked with such vigour, and in such numbers, that their powers of endurance were tested nearly to the breaking strain.

At a very early hour on the morning of the 18th the enemy's snipers occupied the huts on the opposite bank of the river, and were only turned out by two officers who crossed in a sampan and set fire to the village, causing their temporary retirement, and giving the sailors time to throw up breastworks all along the bund. These defences consisted of bales of merchandise of all kinds: wool, silk, cotton goods, sugar, rice, and peanuts,—the sentries' posts among the latter being much sought after, for the peanut is not unpleasant to the taste, and is highly nutritious. At five o'clock a.m. a British officer left in command of an armed train, and in virtual command of 300 Russians, with orders to relieve and bring back the large Russian guard at Chin-liang-Ching; and some two hours afterwards a determined attack was made on the Russians at that station.

The attack took the form of a semi-circle, and the enemy brought 10,000 men and many guns into action. The defence at first consisted of 800 Russians, but at eight o'clock the fighting became so desperate that they sent in for reinforcements. The only force that could be spared for that purpose was two companies of our own bluejackets, who quickly marched up to the threatened point, and deployed on the Russian left.

For four hours the rifle and shell fire was incessant, and though there was abundant cover, the number of casualties was rapidly increasing. The Chinese thought the time had come for an advance, and began to press on the left flank; but our men held their position with the utmost tenacity, and their fire was so steady and effective that no ground was lost. Nevertheless at 2 p.m. the situation was as nearly desperate as possible, and when the Russian guns, in the act of unlimbering, got three beautifully aimed shells right amongst the battery and were forced to retire without firing a shot, it looked as though nothing could save the station.

A gun of sorts was absolutely essential, and it came in the form of a nine-pounder muzzle-loader, a disgrace to the glorious service which at that time had to use them, and which was trundled up by a gun's crew from H.M.S. *Orlando*, by hand. Whatever critics may have said about the weapon, there can only be one verdict about the skill and devotion of the men fated to use it. It was superb. Teed up like a golf ball in front of the platform, the mark of every hostile gun, it was fought to such purpose that it indisputably turned almost certain defeat into a grand victory. To show what the fire was like, it is only necessary to mention that five "Number ones" went down in as many minutes, and at the end of a short half hour, two officers and two men were still working the piece alone. Its fire not only kept down that of several hostile guns, but also effectively checked the advance of the infantry, who were fain to take cover among the numerous mounds to be found over the several acres of ground between the opposing forces.

All chance of a Chinese success was now at an end, and, when the trainload of Russians returned about 4 o'clock, having failed to reach Chin-liang-Ching owing to the destruction of the permanent way, the commanding officer, Colonel Wogack, felt able to take the offensive. The whole force fixed bayonets, and under a withering fire commenced their advance.

On this occasion the enemy did not wait, but, dismayed as much at the stubbornness of the defence as at the impetuosity of the attack, broke and fled through a village in their rear. So disorganised were they that the means of egress became blocked with struggling humanity, and at this point their loss was enormous. The bayonet was employed in clearing the village, and in twenty minutes from the commencement of the advance resistance had ceased. The village was burned and the exulting troops returned to barracks, having administered a salutary lesson to the Chinese. This engagement cost the enemy some 500 killed and wounded: the loss of the allies being 230.

After the action the Russian colonel recognised the gallantry of our men in a kindly speech, in which he said that he had on that day witnessed the traditional pluck and endurance of the British bluejacket, and that he was proud to have commanded such men; further, that he hoped for the sake of civilisation that Great Britain and Russia would always march side by side. The rest of the evening was spent by the one side in building or completing defences, and by the other in mounting guns in closer and more advantageous positions, and when darkness had closed in, all the women and children were sent into the cellars of the town hall, as well as those residents whose houses had already become untenable, or whose position rendered them liable to destruction.

The next day, 19th, was a day of unsuccessful attacks on both sides. It was found that the enemy had mounted two guns on the mud wall to the eastward, which were doing great damage to the British concession, and it became necessary to dislodge them. A force of

130 bluejackets, under Commander Beatty, was told off to operate in conjunction with 400 Russians, and it was decided that our force should deliver the frontal attack at 10.30 a.m., by which time the Russians were to have come up on our left and turned the enemy's right flank. Like many other carefully laid plans, this one miscarried. To begin with, the Russians were late: they delivered a semi-frontal attack instead of carrying out the pre-concerted flanking movement, and finally they lost all touch with our companies.

From that moment the affair became hopeless, the fighting line consisted of but fifty men, who, although they advanced until all their officers were wounded with the exception of one midshipman, were ultimately compelled to retire, having effected nothing. In this disastrous attack Commander Beatty was severely wounded twice in the left arm, and a midshipman also received two wounds which eventually proved fatal. However, it was imperative that those two guns should be silenced, and a 9-pr., the hero of the previous day, was brought in to the bund in front of the Consulate.

During the duel which ensued, Lieut. Wright, the gunnery lieutenant of the *Orlando* was dangerously wounded by a shell which burst almost in his face; his life was despaired of, but he made a miraculous recovery, and lived to receive his well-earned promotion. It is to be deeply regretted that this valuable officer died recently, doubtless from the after effects of his terrible injuries. The 9-pr. was again handled with exemplary skill, and eventually caused the retirement of the enemy, who took their guns with them.

While these events had been going on to the northward of the settlement, similar but opposite movements were taking place to the southward. The Chinese brought guns out of the south gate of the native city, and shelled the west face of the settlements. On being engaged by the two guns on our south-westerly defences, namely another 9-pounder and a 6-pounder Q.F., they turned their attention to our gunners. An artillery engagement ensued which lasted till our magazines, which had been dug in the base of the mud wall, were exhausted, when our two guns ceased fire. This was interpreted by the Chinese as an acknowledgment of defeat, and an attack was made on the emplacement under cover of a bend in the wall.

About 70 Imperial troops got to within 300 yards of the guns under cover, when they rushed towards them, keeping up a brisk fire as they came. Things looked critical, for there was not a single round of ammunition left for the 6-pr., and only three or four for the 9-pr.;

besides which the total force consisted of only one midshipman and eight men. The officer and four men manned the gun; the other four maintained a steady fire with their rifles. A single shrapnel was sufficient; it burst full in the face of the advancing Chinamen, who bolted and were pursued by the remaining rounds until out of range. This finished active operations for the day, which had been slightly in favour of the Europeans.

In view of the probable failure of ammunition and stores, it was determined to endeavour to communicate the existing state of affairs to the outside world. Volunteers were called for, and Mr James Watts, a young Englishman, expressed his willingness to ride through the Chinese forces and make his way to Taku with despatches. None could have been better fitted for the duty. Young, plucky, possessing a perfect knowledge of the country, and possibly the finest rider in the east, Mr Watts undoubtedly had all the qualities necessary for its successful performance. A guard of three Cossacks went with him, and they had one spare horse between them. They started their ride at nightfall, and were seen and pursued almost as soon as they had left the settlement. The alarm was passed from village to village, and it was found necessary to deviate considerably from the line decided upon, in order to avoid the crowds of Chinamen who simply swarmed for some miles round Tientsin.

In one village Mr Watts was recognised, and his name was shouted out, coupled with the most awful threats by the erstwhile servants and grooms who had all become Boxers. Luckily for the little troop, when the Imperial forces had passed, they had firearms to fear no longer, and the most expeditious methods of dealing with the mobs of armed peasants was to charge down on them sword or revolver in hand. The pursuit was kept up till the four horsemen hove in sight of Taku, which was reached safely next morning after a ride of nearly fifty miles.

At dawn on the 20th, the Chinese opened a fierce bombardment, bringing a 2-inch Krupp gun into use for the first time. One of the fifty pound shells from this weapon struck the hospital, and piercing the wall, fell in the passage outside the window of a ward full of wounded officers. Luckily it did not explode, and beyond the shock, which naturally affects one's nerves when lying wounded in bed, no harm was done. During the morning the French settlement suffered very severely from a concentrated shell fire, and by the end of the day there was hardly a habitable house in it. Practically no reply was made by the Allies' artillery, consisting as it did of small and sometimes antique weapons, with a very limited supply of ammunition which was carefully husbanded to stem any rush on the part of the enemy. An attempt was made to silence the 5-inch, by mounting a Maxim on the roof of a house and firing at the flash, but the big fellow took no notice of its puny opponent's angry mutterings, and went on sullenly the whole night.

Next morning the enemy turned their attention to the south-westerly defences again, and when they had tried unsuccessfully to elicit a reply from our two guns in that direction, they vented their spite on the wool-mills, which were held by a midshipman with forty men. These quickly had to leave the buildings, and entrenched in the open in front of them, the midshipman and several men having been wounded by splinters at almost the first discharge.

At half-past ten the mill was set on fire, and blazed furiously, sending up dense masses of black smoke, as the flames caught the large quantities of wool and dye which were stored in the buildings. Machinery to the value of £100,000 was destroyed, and the main building was completely gutted. Immediately the effect of their shell fire became apparent, large masses of troops poured out of the south gate of the city, and it looked as though the Chinese were going to press their advantage. However, at this moment, our two guns woke up, and burst a few shells among them, and on the arrival of our reinforcements, the enemy desisted from further operations, having done considerable damage, but without gaining any military success.

For some time it had been suspected that the enemy had snipers concealed about the settlement itself, and it became amply proved when, in the afternoon, no less than seven were found concealed in a large "godown", all supplied with rifles and a quantity of ammunition. These men were instantly shot, but nothing seemed to check the system of espionage which enabled the Chinese to know the time and meaning of every movement which took place inside the settlement. As certainly as the Europeans fell in, even were it only for the purpose of inspecting arms, so surely did shells commence to fall among the houses around them; and although all spies and signallers who fell into the hands of the allies were summarily dealt with, this annoying power of foresight, which spoilt many a projected surprise, served to harass the defenders, until the native city finally fell into our hands.

The only apparent way of stopping this nuisance seemed to be the expulsion of every Chinaman in the settlement, but as they all professed to be either native Christians or faithful servants, this course of action did not commend itself to the provost marshal. There can be no doubt that if the step had been taken, nine-tenths of them would have been slain, after torture, by their countrymen. On the 22nd June every one was kept in a flutter of excitement all day. In the early morning a courier arrived from Pekin, bringing the news of the death of the German minister, Baron von Kettler, and stating that the Europeans had been ordered to leave within twenty-four hours. The man stated that he was only one of many couriers who had endeavoured to reach Tientsin, and that he knew that two had been caught by the Boxers. He himself had been caught by some Imperial troops, but he had destroyed his message, and they let him go after a close cross examination.

None of the other couriers came in, so it must be supposed that they too were caught, and suffered death for their faithfulness to their European masters. In the afternoon troops were seen advancing from the direction of Taku, and hopes rose high; but heavy firing was heard, and the troops, who were a small force of Russians and Americans, fell back. This naturally caused some disappointment, but it was felt that at last some movement for the relief of the place was on foot, and it was optimistically supposed that the retiring column was merely the advance guard of a powerful force, who would easily overcome the Chinese opposition on the morrow. In the evening the bombardment of the settlement suddenly ceased, and a very heavy fire was heard to the northwestward.

Most of the Chinese guns were withdrawn, and opened fire in the opposite direction; from which it was conjectured that the Admirals' force was returning, and was being hotly engaged some six miles away. The distant firing ceased about eleven o'clock, only to open again furiously at dawn, when the Chinese again bombarded the settlement. Contrary to their usual custom, they failed to attack our outposts in the early morning, and it was generally felt that they were bewildered at the presence of the two forces to the northwestward and south-eastward of them, both of which were feeling for an opening in the cordon. At nine o'clock troops were again seen to be advancing from the south-eastward, and by ten o'clock an engagement was taking place around the Pei-Yang arsenal, and in the villages between this position and the river.

All the troops in the settlement were immediately moved about, to give the enemy the impression that they were about to be attacked in rear, which would have been done had it not been for the Allies' paucity of numbers. At any rate the movement probably bore some fruit, for the Chinese were on the run by eleven o'clock, and by noon a column of 750 British, Americans, and Italians arrived in the German Concession, leaving a force of 1150 Russians and Germans on the other bank of the river.

The Chinese, dispirited at the result of the morning's work, ceased their bombardment, and the first siege of Tientsin was over. What a change had taken place in the short fortnight that the bluejackets had been in garrison. On their arrival they found a busy, prosperous, and pretty European town, whose inhabitants vied with each other in getting up amusements and sports for the men. Prettily dressed women and children were everywhere in evidence, and by their presence greatly added to the success of the various entertainments. The officers were all billeted in the houses of civilians, who appeared to be only too pleased to have them. The English and German clubs both threw open their doors to the visitors, and it was felt on all hands that if this was war, well, "*Vive-la-Guerre.*"

Now, however, trade was at a standstill, and the recreation ground which had recently been prepared for a cricket match, was one of the principal links in the chain of defence. Hardly a house but had been struck by shells, the valuable contents of the warehouses going to form barricades to keep out the bullets which lay thick about every street, and studded every tree and wall. It was indeed a different spectacle. Women and children were to be seen no longer, and the two clubs were both turned into hospitals, which by this time were nearly crowded with wounded officers and men. Instead of the abundance of fresh food which had been the rule, there was now none; bully beef and ship's biscuits had taken the place of fresh mutton and new bread. This is not mentioned as a hardship, but merely to indicate the change that had taken place; for the sailors thrive even in peace time on a certain amount of this substituted diet, besides which they never grumble, so long as they understand the logic of the situation, which in this case was palpable. The first siege was over and the garrison had been reinforced, in fact doubled, but for many days to come there was no certainty about the ultimate safety of the settlements.

CHAPTER 4

Seymour's Dash for Pekin

It will be remembered that Admiral Seymour had suggested that an International Brigade should immediately start for Pekin on the 9th June, and that not only had his colleagues agreed to the step being taken, but had entrusted the command to him. The following account of what took place came from the private diary of a brother officer who served with the column, and is therefore, like the account of most of the other operations, the story of an eyewitness. So many times is one asked the question, "Why ever did Seymour try to relieve Pekin with but 2000 men? Of course the thing was bound to be a failure," that one gets tired of giving the somewhat lengthy explanation necessary to dissipate their ignorance; but enough has been said in the previous chapters to show that no interference was believed possible from the Imperial troops, in which case the force was undoubtedly adequate.

On the Continent the attempt was stigmatized, by one whose eccentricity is well known, as "folly"; but this was not the opinion of his Nationals on the spot, who were well to the fore in all the fighting which took place, and who, by their courage and bearing, set an example unhappily not often followed by some of the other Continental contingents. Apart from this, it must be noted with pride by all Britons, that the first step taken to help the European ministers and the other foreigners in Pekin, originated with one of their own countrymen, who conducted the hazardous enterprise with the greatest intrepidity and skill.

It was believed that two days' work, with a sufficient force, would put the damaged railway line in sufficiently good order to allow of the passage of trains, and on the 10th June five trains started with a total force of 2060 men, composed of British, Germans, Japanese,

Austrians, Americans, French, and Russians. With the force went a few engineers, and any available space was occupied by sleepers and other plant for repairing purposes. On the 10th the trains made about 36 miles' headway, and it was never doubted that the other 50 would be negotiated in a day or two. Repairing the line, however, was found to be killing work; but after a few miles of digging and plate-laying, the pace at which the work was finished increased, and had it not been for the fierceness of the sun and the scarcity of water, still more might have been got out of the men, who seemed to enjoy the novel experience. The bridges, of which there are a good number, were the most difficult to repair; the Boxers had built huge fires underneath them, which not only burnt the sleepers, but warped the rails.

On the 11th, the railway got worse and worse; the rails had been torn up by hundreds of yards, and the permanent way had been destroyed as far as it lay in the Boxers' power. Several small bodies of Boxers were seen in the distance, evidently waiting for the trains to pass by before recommencing operations on the line. All the stations which were passed had been burned and looted, and on arriving at Lo-fa, the Boxers were found in strength. The British from the first train got out and engaged them; several villages were cleared, and forty of the enemy, who fought with fanatical courage although only armed with swords and spears, were slain.

Owing to repeated acts of treachery, it was found necessary to slay all the wounded who did not throw away their arms, several of our men having narrow escapes from men shamming death. All the inhabitants of the surrounding were either Boxers or had decamped, the houses were burnt and looted; grain, kettles, and bowls being among the most useful articles found in them. Owing to the condition of the line, and the little engagement referred to, only 10 miles' progress was made; but there were as yet no pessimistic opinions aired, though as a rule these are common enough at the first sign of difficulties.

On the next day the line was worse still, and it was found impracticable to advance more than a paltry four miles. This put a different complexion on matters, for only two days' provisions had been brought, and recourse was had to the pigs and chickens which were very plentiful in the villages. The well water, in several places, was discovered to be poisonous, and in consequence of the general impurity of all the water to be found, it was all boiled before being used for drinking. Some of the glory of war was infused into the day by decorating the trains banners, which had been captured from Boxers in the

Repairing the line outside Tientsin

Charred sleepers and warped rails on the line outside Tientsin

engagement of the afternoon before; they were nearly all of triangular shape, red in colour, and with various texts and mottoes on them in black characters. A trolley was sent on ahead, manned by eight of our marines, whose duty it was to scout; they got surrounded by mounted Boxers, and killed twenty of them. As usual, the enemy treated rifle fire with supreme indifference, and only fell back on the advance of a company of bluejackets.

On Wednesday the 13th, Lieutenant Smith, the gunnery lieutenant of the *Aurora*, was sent on ahead with fifty sailors, for the purpose of exploring the line, and to guard against surprise. The men were in light marching order and only carried a hundred rounds apiece, with one day's food and water-bottle. After proceeding for two or three miles, they were attacked by about 1800 sword and spearmen. A joss-house was hastily fortified, and six rushes of the enemy were repulsed with heavy loss—about 150. On the retirement of the Chinese for the sixth time, the ammunition was found to be getting low, so the little force withdrew, and fought its way back without any casualties. Unfortunately it was found necessary to abandon the provisions. The whole day was spent in repairing the sidings and line at Lang-Fang, a large and completely ruined station.

A train got through from Tientsin with a welcome mail, and stores of various kinds, and reported that there were signs of the line having been again tampered with in the rear; but that it was expected a good service of trains would soon be running backwards and forwards which would alone suffice to prevent any serious damage being done, unless the Boxers used explosives, of which they did not possess any.

On Thursday, the trains were attacked by 2000 Boxers, who surprised and cut to pieces five Italians on picket duty, who were playing cards instead of keeping watch. On they went, charging Maxims and magazine rifles as though it was an everyday matter; never wavering, never stopping except to go through their bullet-charming gesticulations, they just came on at a trot yelling "*Tow-ah! To-wah!*" (Kill! Kill!) with a calm disregard of death which was as absurd as it was pathetic.

As an officer present with the foremost Maxim said, "It seemed awfully unreal, this mowing down of men but a few yards off." They never got past the first train, whose crew were mainly British. All around it they lay, and just in the wake of the Maxim they lay in heaps. This gun had done its work well, the big leaden bullet crushing, and rendering nerveless, anyone that it hit, whereas the humane nickel-coated bullet failed altogether to stop these pertinacious swordsmen, unless it struck a vital spot.

At last the limit of fanaticism was reached, and the enemy retired, having suffered terribly. Meanwhile a still more hotly contested conflict had been waging at Lo-fa, where Lieutenant Colomb and fifty men had been left in a fortified house, which they called "Fort Endymion" after the name of their ship. They were attacked by 3000 Chinamen, but after some hard fighting, they drove the enemy off with a known loss of 150 killed. An interesting feature of the attack was the bringing of two prehistoric guns into action by the Boxers, from which they fired railway bolts and smooth stones. The first casualties, with the exception of the Italian picket, were caused by these extraordinary weapons; one man being wounded through the right lung by a stone.

On the 15th a train went back, and found that the line in rear of Lo-fa was again completely torn up, and that there was no chance of getting any more news from Tientsin; so the force once more found itself with only two days' provisions, and a quickly diminishing supply of ammunition. Suspicion began to grow that the Regular troops would soon commence active opposition to the advance; and it was felt that, although Pekin would certainly be reached as long as there were only sword and spearmen to contend with, considering the state of the line, it would be well-nigh impossible if the troops abandoned their hitherto neutral attitude. The expected 48 hours to Pekin had already extended to a week; and beyond the fact of having got halfway, and having slain some hundreds of Boxers with practically no loss, the force was in a rather worse predicament than after the first day's work.

On the 16th, the first train retired to Lo-fa, where the garrison of "Fort Endymion" was relieved, and work was commenced again on the rear part of the lines to try and open the all-important communications. By dint of unstinted labour, eight miles were repaired, and Yangtsun was reached again in the evening. The other trains remained at Lang-Fang, and a fortified position near the station was held by German sailors, and christened "Fort Gefion." All private stores were finished, and the service rations were used for the first time. These were eked out with chickens, and the everlasting black pigs which appeared to own no master, and roamed the country at win. Needless to remark, they had not yet developed the man-eating propensities for which they afterwards became noted.

The Yangtsun railway bridge was found to be totally destroyed ;

SEYMOUR'S COLUMN—ARMOURED TRUCK WITH COOLIES

CARRIAGES OCCUPIED BY SEYMOUR'S COLUMN FOR TEN DAYS.

it is the most important bridge on the whole line, being a fine iron structure bridging the Pei-Ho River, half a mile below the town from which it takes its name. On the 18th, those in the first train endeavoured to get everything shipshape for further service. This was satisfactorily accomplished with the exception of perfect cleanliness, which was rendered doubly hard by the total drying up of most of the wells in the vicinity, which obliged one to wash both one's belongings and one's self in the muddy and corpse glutted river. Those who performed the latter operation, in a somewhat squeamish and perfunctory manner, little dreamt that very shortly they would no longer hesitate to wash in it, but would be only too glad to drink it as it was!

In the evening the other trains came down from Lang-Fang, to say that "Fort Gefion" had been attacked, and that Imperial troops had participated in the engagement.

It appears that the German garrison were unexpectedly attacked by 4000 riflemen. Some British and French sailors moved to their assistance, and in the course of some hard hand to hand fighting, 400 Chinese soldiers were killed. The total Allied loss was 6 killed and 48 wounded. At last the blow had fallen, and a foe by no means to be despised had for the first time appeared on the scene.

The task had become well nigh hopeless, and, as the lesser of the two evils, it was decided to retire on Tientsin by way of the river.

A German detachment made a smart capture of some *junks* which were making off, full of railway sleepers, and into them were placed the wounded and what stores were left. The retirement was commenced on Tuesday afternoon, the whole force being on the left bank of the river, and the *junks* being towed by the railway *coolies* and the prisoners. Before starting, all gear, except the food, ammunition, and clothes which the men were wearing, was buried; among other things that were thus lost being the officers' full-dress uniforms, which were brought because it was expected that on the arrival of the force at Pekin there would have been ample occasion to wear them. Three miles' progress was made before dark, the men now proceeding in heavy marching order, with half rations for two days in their haversacks.

The first bivouac was miserable enough; damp mists rose from the river, and in an hour or two's time blankets became saturated, and sleep out of the question. The mosquitoes on the river itself were in countless numbers, and the wounded suffered terribly from their attacks. On the morrow, resistance was met at each village, the enemy, in most cases, being composed of both Imperial troops and Boxers.

SEYMOUR'S COLUMN SERVING OUT GROG

These villages were taken at the bayonet's point, one after another, and the force pushed on as quickly as possible to the next; the same sort of bayonet charge, the same kind of opposition to be overcome, a few casualties on each side, a few captured rifles, and the village was burnt.

This last, although a tiresome and disgusting task, was a military necessity; nevertheless it was a pitiful sight to see old men and women wailing by the side of their burning houses, left to their fate by their younger relations. In no single case were these unfortunates molested by any of the British force, but in one village, where two middle-aged men were captured after having been seen fighting a few minutes previously, two sailors began to thrash them with their fists. This of course was immediately stopped by an officer, who, not understanding the position, began to upbraid the offenders, finishing with words to the effect that the force were not fighting with "peaceful villagers." The men desisted, and having saluted, were walking off, when one remarked:

Yes, I know them peaceful villagers—peaceful villagers wot sells us chickens by day and snipes by night.

During the day, a one-pounder Hotchkiss was captured after the retreat of the enemy, who withdrew it as soon as the charge commenced, and somewhat carelessly hid it in a swamp to the rear of the village.

The Chinese cracker trick, which is really an exceedingly good imitation of heavy independent rifle fire, was used a good deal by the Chinese about this period; but when the first position was taken, of course the burnt crackers told their own tale, and the tremendous fire from the enemy's trenches frightened no one again. Towards evening the Allies made their first acquaintance with the *Jingal*, a weapon on which, until quite recently, even the Imperial troops had placed great reliance; they now formed the Boxers' artillery.

A *Jingal* is nothing more nor less than a huge rifle, fashioned like a modern Mauser without the magazine; they fire a very large leaden bullet, the impulsive force being a proportionately large charge of black powder. Of course their weight makes them too great a load for one man, so they are carried and manned by two, or sometimes three. In some cases the village carpenter had been requisitioned to make them into guns of position, which was done by adopting the swivel system, putting them on the top of large stakes which were firmly driven into the earth.

After another uncomfortable bivouac, the force got under arms again early next morning, and were marching in a long column by the river bank, when a line of cavalry were perceived on the left front about 3 miles off. They were screened by a fringe of trees, and on account of the distance no one was able to make them out sufficiently clearly to be certain of their nationality. However, it was decided from their formation, and the size of their horses, that they were Russian Cossacks. The Russian colours were hoisted, and in answer came a well directed shell, which burst in unpleasant proximity to the Germans. This was followed by others, and, in twenty minutes' time the column found itself heavily engaged with General Nieh's army, 8000 strong, with four batteries. The column was disposed in the following manner; the Germans, Russians, and Japanese were on the right side of the river, and the rest of the force on the left. The natural features of the ground and all important points are mentioned in the account of the battle which follows.

The forces on the left side took cover under a sand bank, and the British cleared No. 1 village and occupied it. It was soon seen that No 2 village was full of the enemy, and as our guns were kept fully occupied by their artillery, so were unable to prepare the assault by shell fire, the British with some Americans therefore again charged and captured it. The Chinese fire at this point was very heavy and well directed, and during the brief rush many casualties occurred, among them being Captain Jellicoe—the British flag-captain, who was dangerously wounded through the lung.

At one time it seemed as though the village would not be taken owing to the want of numbers, but after a slight check, which was made under cover of some banks about 100 yards from the point of attack, the sailors again pressed forward, and the Chinese fled. No time was given to them to prepare No. 3 village, and without a pause the charge was continued, ending in the utter rout of the enemy, with heavy loss.

The allied line by this time consisted of British, Americans, and French, all advancing on the Chinese infantry, with one flank resting on the said sand-bank. The Chinese gradually retired over the other end of it, and from its crest opened a steady fire. Two companies of the *Centurion's* men and some thirty Americans, the whole under the direction of Captain M'Calla, U.S.N. (a fine old Civil War veteran), were sent to turn the enemy's flank, which was done most successfully. The enemy again lost heavily, and had the outflanking force stayed where it was, all would have been well, but the men were kept charging until they found themselves far in advance of the supports, with No. 4 village in front of them, strongly occupied by Imperial troops, and with a heavy fire coming from across the river from tte Chinese position on that side, whose occupants had not yet been evicted by the Russians and Germans.

There was nothing for it but to retire, and with further loss in officers and men, the force managed to extricate itself, with its dead and wounded, from a somewhat delicate position. The battered remnant of those companies were sent to be junk guard, and the fresh men who had at present done nothing were moved up to the fighting line. This advent had an immediate effect, and the Chinese, fighting stubbornly and losing heavily, were pushed back steadily for about 4 miles. A defensive position, the best there was, was chosen for the *junks* and field hospital, and as it was four o'clock in the afternoon, the rear-guard halted, and prepared to bivouac. For three more hours the advance-guard pursued the flying foe, until the men were in danger of becoming exhausted, when the halt was sounded, and they retired on to the already mentioned position.

It is not too much to say that the British did practically all the fighting, and with the exception of the Germans and Americans, the other forces were hardly engaged. The men had been on the march for sixteen hours, twelve of which had been spent in fighting; they were without water to drink, and without time to eat, and even on their return the Pei-Ho was the only refreshment obtainable. Five hours' rest (not for the whole force, for some had to go on picket duty—an arduous task for which some contingents had no great liking), was all that was vouchsafed to the weary men, and at one o'clock next morning the "Fall in" was sounded, and once more the column headed for Tientsin.

By this time there was so little ammunition left for the field guns, that they were all placed in *junks*, and little enough room did it leave for the wounded, whose numbers had been nearly doubled by the previous day's fighting. At 3 a.m. some firing took place in the immediate front, and the marines (British) came upon a Chinese outpost, who after the first few shots fled, leaving their rifles. They had been placed on the outskirts of a small Chinese town, which proved to be absolutely deserted. Sleepy and with empty stomachs, plodding along through the oppressing quietness where all should have been bustle and life, was a weird, uncanny experience. It is on such occasions, in the grey of the early morning, going to who knows what fate, with that awful feeling of expectancy hanging over every one that the nerves get distraught and the imagination, if allowed to wander, makes such jumpy creatures of the finest men; so it was with feelings of relief that the force once more found themselves in the open, and again marching along the river banks.

On leaving the town, the head of the force was challenged from the other side of the river, from what in the puzzling light looked like a wood. An interpreter went forward, and explained that the force was friendly to the Chinese government, and desired nothing better than to be allowed to pass on into Tientsin peaceably. A conciliatory and satisfactory answer was given to this request, and the force was moving on, when suddenly a tremendous artillery and musketry fire was opened on them! Nothing but the darkness saved the head of the column from total annihilation. As it was, however, the force lay down and replied, as well as it was possible, to the tremendous fire from the opposite bank. Just before this happened, the *junk* with the guns foundered, and the others broke adrift, and bid fair to drift right into the middle of the enemy.

Several of the poor wounded were shot again, as they lay in agony fully exposed to the perfect hail of bullets which was poured into them; and it looked as though they would be butchered to a man. However, two splendid men, one from the *Centurion* and one from the *Orlando* swam over the river and succeeded in towing them back to the friendly refuge of a bend in the river, where they at any rate got some shelter afforded by the bank.

One field gun and four machine guns were saved, but five field guns and five machine guns were at the bottom of the river, and thus the force was practically without artillery. In addition to this, most of the foreign contingents were almost out of ammunition, whilst our own stock was rapidly dwindling, till there were only a few boxes in reserve. However, desperate plights are only to be coped with by desperate measures, and it was decided that part of the force should cross the river and charge the arsenal, for such was the enemy's position discovered to be, when objects became distinguishable.

To the comparatively fresh Russians the task was offered, but the honour was refused, and eventually the whole of the British marines with 40 bluejackets were led over the river above the bend, and prepared for the assault. There was cover available up to 200 yards of the arsenal walls, and such was the surprise of the Chinamen at seeing some 200 marines and sailors advancing at the double, cheering lustily, that they deserted the northern wall almost before they could fire a shot. In the meantime the German sailors had moved down opposite to the river gate of the arsenal, and by their fire, managed to keep under that of the enemy's field pieces from that direction. Fighting of the fiercest description took place inside the enclosure, and for some time the British barely held their own, possessing neither the numbers nor the local knowledge of the enemy, who were able to harass them considerably from buildings and other positions which our men did not understand how to get at, because of the somewhat complicated arrangement of the houses and moats, which were here, there, and everywhere in the arsenal grounds.

After about an hour's hard fighting, the place was cleared, and the enemy's guns were manned by our men and turned on to a village about a mile away, into which the majority of the defenders had escaped. Desultory fighting also took place on the left bank of the river, and it was not until 3 p.m. that the whole force had crossed, and had got the various positions assigned to them. Before this had happened, the small British garrison had to repel repeated attempts made by the Chinese infantry to retake the place; the Chinese loss in their several advances being great. The first care, when the enemy finally retired, was for the wounded, and these were all placed in as comfortable quarters as could be found in the existing circumstances.

By four o'clock it was recognised what a prize had been captured. It was a military store known as the Hsi-Ku arsenal, being about a mile in circumference, along the whole length of which ran a mud wall about 15 feet high and 12 feet broad on the top. The store-houses were at the south end of the enclosure, and by virtue of a high brick wall which enclosed them, were made into an inner line of defence. Other houses were scattered here and there, and were used as temporary barracks, etc. Confidence was completely restored by this successful capture, and it was felt that had there been a sufficiency of food and ammunition, the column might make an almost indefinite resistance.

Friday night passed comparatively quietly, but at daybreak on Saturday the Chinese made another determined attack. They actually charged right up to the south-west corner, and some even got into the long rushes inside the embankment. Some marines, under Captain Beyts of the *Centurion*, were marching to take up their positions on the wall when they were surprised by these daring spirits, and in the hand-to-hand fighting which followed, this officer was unfortunately slain. The main attack was beaten off, but the enemy did not cease to threaten others until about eleven o'clock.

At the first opportunity, the stores were examined, and to the inestimable delight of all, there was found in them 15 tons of rice, an almost unlimited supply of medical comforts and stores (which had run out with the allies so completely that the *pugarees* from the officers' and marines' helmets had all been used for bandages), besides forty-five .303-in. Maxims, with 7,000,000 rounds of ammunition, thousands of Mannlicher repeating carbines and rifles (also with ammunition), and large numbers of excellent quick-firing field guns, which included two pom-poms. The discovery was of such value that it was difficult for one to believe one's own eyes. Here was Lee-Metford ammunition enough to last the British force for months; modern repeating rifles sufficient to re-arm all the rest of the force whose ammunition was low—which was immediately done—guns, and machine guns, in such numbers that it would have been possible to mount one at every fiftieth yard; and food which, though it was better suited to the Chinese stomach than to that of Europeans, nevertheless, would serve to keep the whole force alive for some weeks.

One of the miserable sand-storms, which occur with some frequency in the summer months in this district, raged all Saturday afternoon, greatly adding to the general discomfort. Nothing had been heard from Tientsin, now only just above six miles distant, and it seemed as though the force would have to stand a somewhat lengthy siege. During the afternoon a well was dug, from which the men were able to get some comparatively good drinking water, for the first time for days; the only other work that was done being the mounting of guns, and the removal of the wounded into the now empty field-gun store. At night rockets were fired and blue lights burned, but no response came from Tientsin, and it was feared that the settlements were in as dire need as the admiral's column.

That the country swarmed with troops was known from the story of a wounded prisoner, who admitted that the attempts to re-take the place had been made with twenty-five battalions (nominally) 500 men in each, but probably of not more than 300 to 400, and that the troops were much discouraged at their non-success and heavy losses. The last attack had been pressed with the utmost determination, and European tactics had been employed throughout. The troops employed were men with a reputation second only to that of the Shantung army, which is commanded by that able and clear-sighted viceroy, Yuan-Shi-Kai; and it speaks volumes in their favour that they should have fought as well as they did, after their enormous losses in the previous engagements.

On Sunday morning the defence was rearranged, the British and Germans sharing the three most dangerous walls, the Americans and Russians the fourth wall, while the French and Japanese did sentry work, picket duty, and defended the inner line. Some tents were discovered, and were pitched forthwith; they afforded a welcome shelter from the sand which penetrated everywhere else. The enemy amused themselves with a long-range fire until ten o'clock, when they attacked the Americans and Russians on the north front. Their fire caused several casualties among the British on the west bank, entirely enfilading them, so the greater part of them reinforced the Americans, and in a short time the attack recoiled and fizzled out. Their snipers, however, were very busy all day, and it was only by choosing picked shots and placing them in advantageous positions that the men could get any rest from their annoying fire.

In the afternoon, the native city and some forts further down the river were vigorously shelled, but they appeared to be busily engaged in the opposite direction, and only occasionally replied. The wounded were given a treat in the shape of some horseflesh for dinner; it had belonged to a Chinese officer, who was shot with his horse during the morning's attack. It was unfortunate that no more was procurable, for the wounded numbered 230, and what is one horse among so many?

The total losses up to date had been 62 killed and 230 wounded, including—British, 27 killed, 97 wounded; Germans, 12 killed, 62 wounded; Russians, 10 killed, 27 wounded; Americans, 4 killed, 28 wounded; Italians, 5 killed, 3 wounded; Japs, 2 killed, 3 wounded; and French, 1 killed, and 10 wounded, out of an original force of 2066, composed of British 915, Germans 450, Russians, 312, French 158, Americans 112, Japanese 54, Italians 40, Austrians 25.

Day broke on Monday 25th without any alarm, and the only signs of the enemy were a small force of infantry, and a strong column of cavalry, who were descried at the other side of the railway embankment.

At about half-past eight, two of the forts down the river were seen to be shelling in a direction neither towards the settlements nor Seymour's arsenal, and it was conjectured that a relief force was coming at last. Seymour immediately shelled the forts and native city vigorously, trusting or desiring to assist the hoped-for relievers, and managed to draw the fire of two or three guns on to his own position. At half-past nine, sharp rifle fire was heard, and the Chinese cavalry were seen to retire, followed by their infantry, who did not appear to take any part in the engagement; and shortly afterwards the head of a European column was seen; advancing unmolested across the plain on the other side of the river in the direction of the arsenal.

Half an hour after this the forces had joined hands, and thus a march, which, if only for the gallantry of the men and resource of the officers who made it, deserves to remain famous, was rapidly drawing to what was perhaps only a semi successful conclusion. The attempt to reach Pekin had failed, but the great damage done to the enemy, both in human life and in warlike stores, together with the immensely difficult but masterly withdrawal, served to almost turn the scale in favour of the Europeans.

CHAPTER 5

Operations for the Relief of Tientsin

The days following the forcible occupation of the Taku Forts were spent in destroying all useless and superfluous Chinese stores, such as small-arm ammunition, loose powder, or shells for the guns, which were too old for use; in fact any war material which might prove useful to the Chinese in the very improbable event of the forts again changing owners. The South forts were occupied by the Russians and Germans, the North fort by the Japanese, and the North-west fort by the British and the twenty-five Italians who had fought in the line with our men on the day before.

More gruesome work than the destruction of stores had first to be attended to. The Chinese dead, some of them hideously mutilated by shell fire, had to be buried, and the necessary hurry with which this was carried out, rendered it impossible to do it in a more decent manner than to throw their corpses into the river. In addition to this work, the forts had to be put into a state of defence, as it seemed impossible to imagine that the Allies would be left in peaceable possession of the much vaunted "impregnable Taku Forts"! All modern guns not seriously damaged were prepared for instant use, and when necessary, fresh magazines were dug for each of them. The magazines were perhaps the one radically bad part of the internal arrangements, and it will be remembered that two had been exploded during the bombardment.

Even more important than defensive qualities were the health and cleanliness of the men, and steps were immediately taken to ensure both. All rubbish and dirt, of which there was a supply now too great for the demand, but which had decreased with the change of masters, was burnt. A new system of washing was arranged, and the cleanest houses were used as barracks. The officers took the Chinese officers' quarters, and an idea may be got of the state of the other buildings when it is stated as a fact, that sleep, even in the officers' rooms, was quite impossible on account of the numberless specimens of the nimble flea. Water and provisions were easily obtained from the fleet, and all water-communications being now open, the procuring of these luxuries soon became a matter of mere routine.

The life was not altogether without excitement. On the first evening the Japanese did not turn up to take over their fort, so forty-four English bluejackets had to go and pretend to defend a position nearly half a mile in circumference. Naturally their position was the cause of the greatest anxiety to Commander Craddock, who was indefatigable in his efforts, and was busy all night mounting Maxims, getting ammunition, and making plans with the commanders of the gunboats to repel any possible attack. However, no attack was made, and the Japanese arrived during the next day.

One evening during this period, some nervous Italian sentry discovered an imaginary enemy, and for some time after the report of his rifle, and the hasty retreat of the foe (a dog), one of the gunboats—not the *Algerine*!—indulged in heavy gun practice at apparently nothing! As one can imagine, this kind of life began to pall on men who were eager to see more fighting, and all hands heartily wished that the much talked of advance to Tientsin would commence. Of this there seemed to be but little likelihood, for the total forces at the disposal of the Allies did not exceed a thousand men, and even then, a garrison for the forts had to be deducted from this number, in addition to which there seemed to be a very general idea that the detachments at Tientsin were having a right royal time of it; or even supposing that they were fighting, they were in all probability capable of looking after themselves.

So much for ideas, which were not allowed to last long, for one morning Mr Watts rode in with his dispatches, which explained the desperate fight the garrison were maintaining, and asked for more men, more guns, and more ammunition. The authorities, already rather alarmed by the somewhat incoherent yarn of the men who had tried to come down in the *Spray*, immediately grasped the situation, and the *Terrible* happily arriving at the same time as a shipload of Russians, a relief force was forthwith formed. The adventures of the *Spray* party had been extraordinary. At the time when urgent need of communicating with the outside world became manifest, these brave fellows, seven in number, volunteered to take a little steam launch and endeavour to run the gauntlet by river. They seemed doomed to failure at the outset, for they ran ashore, and stuck fast when only just a few miles past the lines of the Chinese army. All their efforts to get the boat off were unavailing, and in due course they were discovered by some Boxers, who immediately went off to rouse the neighbourhood.

When night fell there were quite a large number of these bloodthirsty gentlemen on the bank, and it was decided that it was better to desert the boat than to fight with practically no chance of success. Accordingly, taking advantage of the gloom caused by the disappearance of the moon behind some clouds, the whole party slipped quietly over the gunwale, and swam to the opposite bank to that on which they could just distinguish the Boxer sentries. Hardly had they done so when the Boxers dispatched a body of men over to the stranded launch, and, having poured paraffin all over it, set it ablaze. By means of this light the fugitives were spotted, and an extraordinary chase ensued. Luckily the Boxers were absolutely without firearms, while the little party were all armed with rifles and bayonets, without which all of them would doubtless have been killed within an hour or two.

The distance to Taku from where the Europeans had landed was about twenty-five miles, but this was quite doubled eventually, by the necessity of having to avoid villages and other parties of Boxers, which were to be seen in all directions. The narrowest escape of all the many that befell this little band, occurred when in desperation they hid in a large clump of rushes to get some rest.

Evidently they were suspected of being in the vicinity, however, and a party of Boxers searched the rushes, thrusting their pikes into all likely corners, but luckily without discovering the runaways. An attempt to get food also nearly proved disastrous. One of the civilians, who used to shoot a great deal in the neighbourhood, said he knew a Chinaman whom he had often befriended, and who would perhaps give them some native cakes and tea. On arriving at his hut, however, and making his request, backed by the promise of many dollars, the man turned scarlet with rage, and said, "What? tea and cakes indeed, why I'm going to kill you"; and immediately sped off in the direction of the nearest village to get assistance. After many other similar vicissitudes, the party arrived at Taku on the morning of the 20th in an utter state of collapse.

To revert to the relief force: The *Terrible* had on board 300 Royal Welsh Fusiliers, and 40 of the Royal Engineers; and these, with 250

Royal Welsh Fusiliers leaving H.M.S. "Terrible"
on board the "Fame"

English bluejackets from the Northwest fort, and 23 Italians, entrained for Tientsin on June 21st under the command of Commander Craddock. An hour or two previously, about 1000 Russians, 150 Americans, and 250 Germans had entrained for the same destination, bringing the total force up to just 2000 men.

With the British train was a specially constructed water tank, and provisions sufficient to last five days. Bad luck pursued the train from the beginning, for not five miles from Tong-Ku the engine left the rails, and a mishap occurred which might have had extremely serious consequences. In the course of its erratic wanderings the engine upset the first two trucks, on one of which was the water tank, the other being full of officers and men. The damage to human life and limb was happily nil, beyond a few more or less severe contusions, but the precious water tank had to be left, and it was only by dint of hard work, and the loss of a couple of hours' time, that the expedition was able to resume its journey.

Without further incident the train arrived at a point eighteen miles from Tientsin, where the line had been slightly destroyed, passing on their way the garrison of Russians at Chin-Liang-Ching. This place, it will be remembered, had previously been the object of a train expedition from Tientsin which failed at first owing to the state of the line, but which had succeeded at length in reaching it. They had remained undisturbed during the whole of the past very exciting week. Here the force spent the night, and received the news that the Russians and Americans, who had attempted to push their way through to the settlements without waiting for the British, had been defeated and repulsed with the loss of an American machine gun and some men.

The next morning the force was engaged in clearing all the neighbouring villages, which were full of Boxers. These it was not safe to leave on the rear of the column's advance, which had been fixed for the morrow (23rd). The trains also managed to get six miles nearer Tientsin, reducing the distance to be marched to twelve miles. On the same day another train left Tong-Ku with two 6-pr. Q.F. guns, a quantity of ammunition and provisions, and with orders to convey details to the respective forces. It was a mixed crew who took their places in it; five British, with a naval engineer officer running the engine, five American marines, and seven Russians, the whole under the charge of an English midshipman. They stopped at the scene of the disaster of the previous day, and took on board the eleven men who had been clearing the line, and who had done wonders, even to the righting

AUTHOR AND DETACHMENT FROM H.M.S. "BARFLEUR" FOR DUTY
IN TIENTSIN

"FAME" LANDING ROYAL WELSH FUSILIERS

of the overturned water cart. Some six miles further on Boxers were seen burning the line; fortunately they did not see the train until too late, when they bolted into some rushes near the line. A lesson was necessary, so the train was stopped, the midshipman and several men detrained and, after a short search, discovered and slew one of the delinquents, who had a can of oil on his person besides several boring implements for damaging the sleepers. From the moment of restarting till Chin-Liang-Ching was reached, nothing happened worthy of recording; but on arriving there those in the train could for the first time hear continuous firing, and the burning villages, and dense clouds of smoke, proved to be an infallible index to the position of the main body.

On reaching Commander Craddock's force, which had just returned from a hard day's skirmishing, the men were engaged in cooking a meal preparatory to a few hours' rest before the advance next morning. The position chosen for the night's bivouac was a splendid one. On the right was the railway embankment and a canal, in front was another canal spanned by a substantial bridge, on the left was a high bank, and in rear was a village which unfortunately was burning. The Russians and Germans under Major-General Stoessel were two miles in advance, and lay in the open; but the English and Americans, after having first seen to the comfort of their officers, built themselves extremely comfortable shakedowns. During the day a Mohammedan priest had been captured, and on being assured of his safety, told Mr Watts, who was returning to Tientsin in the capacity of guide and interpreter to the column, that eight miles in front lay General Ma and 15,000 of the most efficient Imperial troops; which piece of news seemed likely to militate largely against the expressed intention of dining in Tientsin on the morrow.

The only diversion during the night was a pleasant surprise. The camp was roused about midnight by a train's whistle, and it proved to be 150 men of the 1st Wei-Hai-Wei regiment, and a 12-pr. Q.F. gun under Lieutenant Drummond of H.M.S. *Terrible*. Having detrained, the Chinese regiment accompanied the force when they started at 3 a.m. on the 23rd; a guard of about fifty men and the gun being left behind to guard the camp, so that there might be somewhere to fall back on in case of a reverse.

The British and Americans and Italians were on the left side of the railway embankment, and when in extended formation, their left flank rested on the river bank, where several villages were situated,

"Terrible" 12-pr Q.F. gun on improvised mounting used at the relief of Ladysmith

which had to be cleared on the way. The Russians and Germans deployed on the other side of the railway, in a large plain which extends from the coast nearly to Pekin, and with them went their artillery, a six-gun battery; the only gun on the British side being a 12-pr, from the American man-of-war *Monocacy*. As usual the transport was the great difficulty, and the officer in charge expresses himself as follows:

The arrangements, although as good as possible under existing circumstances, were meagre in the extreme; I can speak feelingly on this matter. I happened to be in charge of the *impedimenta*, which, although it only consisted of a big water cart and a heavy load of ammunition, and could be stowed on two Pekin carts, was nevertheless much too heavy for the mule and the donkey which were the only beasts of burden obtainable. In a civilised country I should have certainly been summoned by the Society for the Prevention of Cruelty to Animals, for the mule had been more or less severely wounded by a bullet, and eventually died. However, war is hardly a civilised game, and I determined to do my best.

Before a mile had been passed the convoy—a high-sounding title, which in this case applied to myself, two men, and two beasts—had grown extremely unpopular with the commanding officer, who can have had no idea of the difficulties to be contended with; and had, in addition, fallen half a mile astern of the fighting line, owing to the incapability of the united efforts of us three men and the two animals to drag the carts through sand nearly up to the axle bars. From our point of view the situation was first ludicrous and then alarming; from the commanding officer's standpoint, it must have been more than aggravating the whole time, for he was a man who took the greatest trouble to perfect every detail conducive to success, and had in this case been baulked by the necessity for quick action, which rendered it impossible to improve on the existing arrangements.

Before we had gone four miles, a desultory musketry fire was heard on the right, which soon increased to a tolerably heavy fusillade. As yet the main advance was unimpeded, but as no forward movement became apparent from the wing on which the firing was going on, and as it was essential that touch should be kept along the whole line, it was decided to await developments in that quarter. By this time we were almost out of sight of the fighting line, and a bad sand-storm was sweeping in our faces.

Suddenly a mounted man was seen to cross the railway embankment and gallop in our direction. He proved to be a Cossack, who by his gestures seemed to want us to reinforce some one. Perhaps we were mistaken; perhaps he was the possessor of a pretty wit, or the third alternative suggests itself, perhaps he was mad. At any rate I pointed to my two men, and violently shook my head, then to the mule (now just at the point of death) and said "can do," whereat the Cossack seemed offended, and then as a few men commenced to snipe at us, I lured him off his pony, took his place, and galloped off to report the situation to Commander Craddock. He very kindly rode back with me, and instructed me as to the best path to take, and gave me instructions to do the best I could for my convoy.

I accordingly got permission from the major in command of the fusiliers to take an officer and twelve men of his regiment, and a similar number of Royal Engineers under Lieutenant Browne, R.E., as a rearguard. These were perforce turned into packhorses, and we started again. In about two minutes from our new start one of the escort got a bullet through the knee, and added materially to the weight of the ammunition cart until a stretcher was got for him, when we at last picked up the force, who were temporarily checked opposite the Pei-Yang arsenal.

We found that the Germans and Russians had tried to take this position, but had been repulsed and driven over on to our side of the railway line. From the embankment their guns vigorously shelled the arsenal, and so far succeeded in keeping down the enemy's fire, as to allow of our men crossing a canal, and continuing their advance. From this moment the state of the roads was so much better, that we managed to keep our proper distance from the firing line, and the thirsty men refilled their water bottles at the first halt.

Underneath the bridge nearest to the arsenal, the Chinese had placed two 500lb. observation mines, upon which two tired American marines thought fit to sit; but the Chinese did not explode them, and the wires were cut before any damage was done.

It now became impracticable for the German and Russian troops to continue their advance along the right of the line, as they would have been in the open, with a hostile force of three times their number operating on their right flank, as well as being subjected to the fire from the field guns in the arsenal; so they covered the advance of the rest of the force who were engaged with the enemy in some entrenched villages in front. The Chinese were in force and under excellent cover, when suddenly the red ensign was distinguished flying over the Tientsin town hall, the sight of which proved to be a magnificent stimulant to the allies. Several men fell in the open, but the village was rushed without heavy loss, and the work of clearing the streets was begun.

For some time it was warm work, and two companies of our sailors were placed in a difficult position from which they were cleverly extricated. As the men passed through the village it was burnt, which completely nullified the possibility of an attack in the rear, and as the houses began to grow fewer, and the open country appeared, the Imperial troops broke and fled. The few last streets were like a battue, and in this instance the much vaunted fearlessness of the Boxers, who at last had the courage to remain to the end, was severely tested.

Some fanatics certainly "came" for the companies with swords, and one man had the temerity to hurl a "stinkpot" at a lieutenant, but these were quite the exceptions, and were quickly dispatched. For the most part the Boxers had remained only to run at the last, or die; often the former, more often both. Quarter was neither asked for nor given, for in the Boxer proclamations were passages relating to European women and children which put them on a par with incarnate devils without human feelings.

At length the work was finished, and once more the men left the village for the open. But before departing two incidents happened, one pathetic, the other weird. An old man was led right down the fire-swept street towards one of our companies by a little boy aged about four. The poor old fellow was blind, and his grandson seemingly preferred to trust our men rather than anyone else. Who knows? perhaps he was right. Needless to say he was unharmed, and led out of the burning village safely. In the other case, a bluejacket just about to bayonet a man in the back, who had rushed at him with a sword and then fled, remarked, "No, I'm blowed if I do, it's a dirty way of doing it," and shot him instead.

When clear of the village the settlements were in full view, and

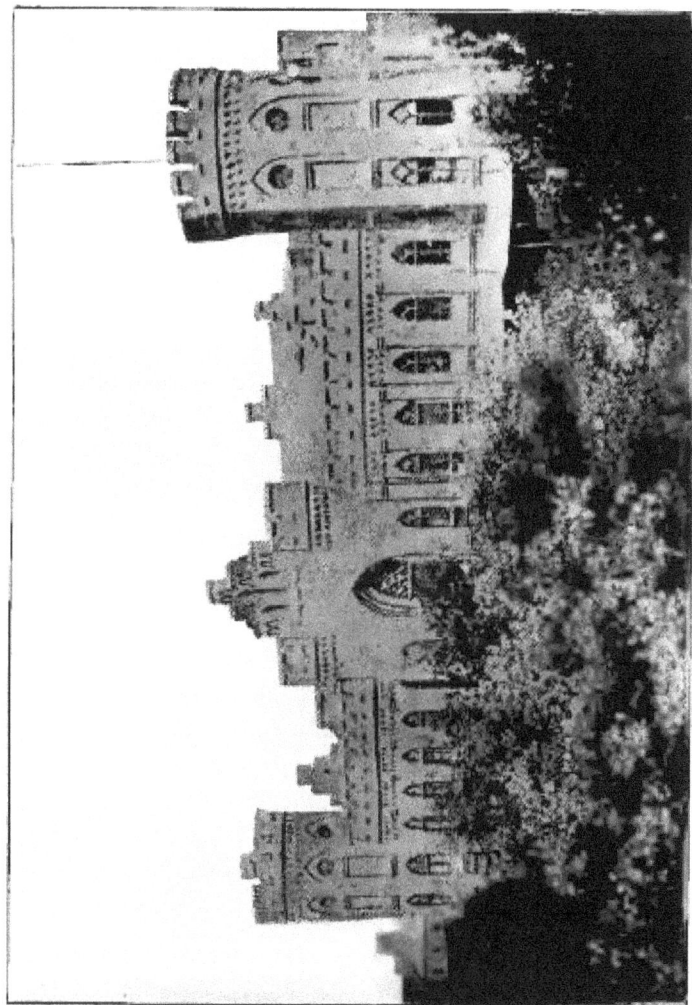

TIENTSIN TOWN HALL

the intervening mile or so was soon passed. Some of the staff crossed the river in *sampans*, while the rest of the force made their way up the bank, and arrived at the ruined military college, just in time to catch the last of the Imperials, who were by this time in full flight from our extreme right, where they had attempted to rally on deserting the left and centre. A raft of logs was swung over the river, and the tired but elated men scrambled over into the relieved town, amid cheers and general congratulations. The pleasure of the meeting was mutual, for it was doubted if the garrison could hold out so long, in addition to which, the gratification of the relieving force, at meeting old ship-mates and friends, was quite as keen as that of the defenders.

The twelve miles had been traversed in eight hours, which seems an unconscionably long time, when the fact of the fighting, not having been very severe, is taken into consideration. But it must be remembered that the ground over which the march had taken place was mainly sand, that a blinding sand-storm had been blowing in the men's faces, and that the opposing force was greatly superior in point of numbers and position. Only those who have experienced a heavy sand-storm in the middle of a hot summer day, can sufficiently appreciate the second cause of our tardy march.

In view of the after events, "The relief of Tientsin" seems almost a misnomer, but by this action much-needed guns and reinforcements had been brought in, and the communications to Taku had been cleared, and henceforth, through the military incapacity of the Chinese generals, they remained open.

The Russians encamped on the left bank of the river, and, in consequence of their presence, the station could in future only be attacked from two sides instead of three. Instead of the terrible uncertainty which the Allies had felt about themselves on the day before, there was now a conviction that the eventual relief of Pekin was only a matter of time. But as Seymour was still unheard of, and his whereabouts unknown, his relief would evidently have to be their next task.

TIENTSIN AGAIN PEACEFUL

CHAPTER 6

The Relief of Seymour

The remainder of that day, and the whole of the next, were spent in complete rest. After the events of the last week, it seemed difficult to realise that anything out of the ordinary was afoot. There was no shelling, no attack on the outposts—in fact nothing but the everlasting sniping during the hours of darkness, which merely ensured the watchfulness of the sentries. Women were again seen about the streets, and a few little children walked about with the air of supreme indifference to their strange surroundings. Every one knew that this was only a lull before the storm of the bombardment, and another siege; but it was felt that the worst was over, and that the Chinese blockade would never again be as effective as heretofore.

Relievers and relieved met and exchanged experiences at the bar of the German club, which was still open, and of which all officers became honorary members. Dinner parties were given by the lucky ones whose stores of tinned luxuries had not already vanished, it being rightly held that it was well to make the most of the impromptu truce, which existed only that the Chinese might collect enough morale to again assume the offensive. In the evening the *Terrible* 12-pr. came in, escorted by a small body of the Hong-Kong regiment, who arrived at the relieving force's last camp only a few hours after the commencement of the advance. This regiment is composed almost entirely of Pathans, who were enlisted in India for service at Hong-Kong. Their arrival at this stage of the operations enabled them to claim to be the first Indian troops on the spot; but as a matter of fact there were twelve Sikh policemen in Tientsin, who all volunteered for military service, and took part in the recent defence.

On the 24th June a native runner got through from the commander-in-chief, and his news was to the effect that the admiral was in

Hsi-Ku arsenal, hard pressed, and with many wounded. He requested a force of 2000 men to extricate him. This message was more cheering than many had dared to hope for. Nearly everyone had given the admiral's party up for lost, the best that they had hoped for being that he might be shut up in Pekin with his force, and in all probability be undergoing the same kind of mental anxiety that had lately befallen themselves. However, Hsi-Ka was only six miles away, and it was believed to be a defensive position of great strength.

A force of the required strength was immediately raised and organised, it was composed as follows: Russians 1000, with three Maxims and two guns; British 600, with two Maxims; and 300 Americans, Germans, Japanese, and Italians, making the total within a hundred of 2000. Colonel Shirinsky, a Russian officer of some distinction, was in command of the whole force, and he decided that the various contingents should rendezvous at his camp at midnight, intending to make a night march and attack the enemy, who were expected to offer a stem opposition at dawn. In the evening the 12-pr. and a 6-pr. shelled the western arsenal, known as the Hi-Kuan-Su, and set it on fire, several unimportant explosions taking place in consequence of the proximity of houses containing ammunition. The departure of the column took place from the town hall at 11.15 p.m., and was quite affecting, the British moving off first, amid feminine cheers and cries of "Good luck," "Mind you bring him back," closely followed by the Americans.

Some difficulty was experienced in crossing the river, for the bridge, which the Russians had promised to have ready, was not nearly finished, and it proved to be a risky business getting over the half planked-in *junks* in the darkness. Another delay was caused on the other side by the stupidity and carelessness of the guide, who lost his way at the very beginning of the march, and took some time to correct his mistake. However, the rendezvous was reached about 1 a.m., and fortunately the Russians had themselves only just taken up their positions. From their camp the rays of the gunboats' searchlights were plainly visible in the mouth of the river thirty miles away, and a bluejacket remarked laughing, that it showed fellow-feeling "for them chaps to try and light us on our way." In a quarter of an hour the combined force moved forward, and for about a mile and a half skirted the mud wall, when they tinned off into the country in the supposed direction of the bridge over the Lutai Canal.

After marching in this direction for some time without finding it, it became evident something was wrong, so a halt was called, and the Russian colonel sent out a reconnaissance party to ascertain its whereabouts. It turned out that it had been passed unnoticed on the left flank, and was about half a mile in rear of the force, so the men had to retrace their steps. But on reaching it, it was found to have been made almost impassable for infantry, and it was soon evident that the Russian guns would have to remain behind; in fact there were grave doubts about the practicability of getting even the Maxims over.

Search parties immediately moved up and down the canal banks, and returned with two sampans, which solved the difficulty of the men's passage, and it was found that the two together were capable of transporting the Maxims also. The Russian sappers, too, helped to replace planks and sleepers on the wrecked iron frames of the bridge itself, and the passage did not occupy more than an hour altogether. It was not, however, effected quite peaceably, for the force was spotted by two of the little land forts near the river, about two miles away, and these promptly opened fire on the bridge with four guns. Their shooting, however, was high, and the shrapnel were bursting in a cemetery to the rear. If the Chinese had known this they would have probably ceased firing, as the spirits of their ancestors are nearly sacred to them. As it was, such ancestral spirits as were in that cemetery must have rested uneasily that morning, and bemoaned their fate at this un-looked for visitation of the "great north wind," or some other similar fantasy.

An interesting incident happened when the crossing was about half finished. The torpedo lieutenant of H.M.S. *Endymion* rode to-wards the forts to find out if possible something about the strength and position of the enemy, when suddenly some twenty Chinamen fired at him from behind cover at a distance of not more than 30 yards. Their nerves, however, must have been in a wretched condition, for he was not even touched, and the only thing for him to do seemed to be to ride straight at them, which he did, whereupon they straightway bolted, leaving one man a prisoner in his hands.

Here of course was a fund of information ready to hand, but there was no interpreter nearer than the main body, now some 600 yards away behind a massive embankment. Accordingly this young officer made it clear to his prisoner in a way that naval officers can do, even without an interpreter, that he wished him to run by his stirrup or take the consequences, and then started to canter slowly back. But the Chinese who had fled recovered from their fright, and proceeded to open fire on him as he retired. For some minutes there was no result, when suddenly they managed to hit their comrade, who fell shot through the leg, the officer safely regaining shelter under a brisk fire. The wounded Chinaman after this, one can imagine, did not hold the prowess of his fellow soldiers in much respect, and who can blame him. War is sufficiently exciting at all times, without any necessity for being shot by one's friends, to render it more so.

When the whole column had crossed the canal, the men rested under cover of the railway embankment, while the Russian scouts reconnoitred the country ahead. No reply was made either to the enemy's shell fire or to their now pretty heavy musketry fire, both of which were harmless to our perfectly invisible companies; but the two Russian guns, which had to remain behind, were ordered to find a position from which to knock out some of the hostile guns. After a short "stand easy," the scouts returned with the news that the road was open, with the exception of a strong body of cavalry, who were slowly retiring about 2 miles away. Advancing about 300 yards further, the head of the column came to a gap in the embankment which exposed it to a warm fire. The Russians crossed first, the British next, and then the Germans and Americans. Therein were several casualties, but surprisingly few considering the range—only some 500 yards.

Another half mile and the cover again came to an end, the British arriving at the dried-up river bed just in time to see the final retreat of the Chinese cavalry, and to hear stentorian cheers from the Russians, who had discovered that the cluster of trees on the plain on the left front was no other than our lost admiral's position. This was indeed good news. Some excitement was caused by the appearance of seven Chinese mounted scouts in an Osier bed on the left, who, however, on being discovered, galloped safely off with the exception of one man, who together with his horse was shot after an enormous expenditure of ammunition.

On leaving the river bed the force marched in five long lines towards the arsenal, the intervals between the men being about five paces. The Chinese gunners, who had expended a quantity of ammunition with no effect whatever, now entirely failed to grasp the situation, and instead of shelling the necessarily large target in the open plain, proceeded to turn their guns on to Seymour's arsenal with some result. In a few minutes, however, the British, German, and Italian ensigns were plainly distinguishable, and it became apparent that the least half of the relieving party's arduous mission, that of reaching the besieged admiral, was practically accomplished. By ten o'clock the two forces were exchanging cheers across the river to the accompaniment of segment shell from the Chinese, and five minutes later the commanding officers of the various contingents were conversing with their Nationals among the besieged force, while the commanding officers of the two columns were already arranging for the withdrawal.

Meetings such as these are rather overpowering, there is so much to be said, such a lot of hand-shaking, which is all the worse because of the amount of real pleasure put into the grip, and such numbers of friends to be congratulated, that the conversation rarely gets beyond "Hallo, old man. Awfully glad you're still going," from the reliever; and from the relieved, "Thanks, old chap, very pleased to see you; but I say, have you got a cigarette on you? I've not had a smoke for days!" And having lighted up, they proceed, by some tacit understanding, to discuss any other subject in the world except the past and future slaying of Chinamen. It had been hoped to get back to Tientsin before dusk, but this was found to be out of the question, owing to the lack of transport for the wounded, and other difficulties which could not be overcome on the spur of the moment; so it was decided to commence the retirement at 2.30 a.m. next morning.

It was soon seen that, although the enemy had allowed the relieving column to arrive almost without opposition, they were not going to allow the Europeans to effect all the necessary preparations for their coming departure, without making themselves as objectionable as possible. The arsenal was shelled without ceasing by the hostile guns in the land forts and native city, and at eleven o'clock a hitherto unnoticed force commenced a most harassing long-range fire from a position on the railway embankment. An attempt was made to dislodge them by Maxim fire, and with this object three Russian Maxims each deliberately fired a long belt of ammunition without stopping, at an invisible object about 2000 yards away, needless to say without having the desired effect. So a mixed force, mostly British, were sent out to dislodge the intruders, which was promptly done.

Unfortunately there were several casualties among the Russians and the Royal Welsh Fusiliers, who had to advance across half a mile of perfectly flat plain before the Chinese took themselves off. After this, strong pickets were posted all along the railway fine, and the work of making a pontoon bridge, to allow the passage of the wounded, was quietly proceeded with.

In the meantime the Russian colonel on the other side of the canal, to minimise the risk of being attacked on the return march on the morrow. Not only was this done, but our 12-pr. in Tientsin succeeded in silencing two guns which, it was seen, might harass the retirement. The effect of this was excellent. While the wounded were being conveyed across the river to be put under the friendly shelter of an enclosed graveyard close by, other parties were shelling the surrounding villages and forts, in order to ensure a quiet night from sniping; while yet a third party under the gunnery lieutenant of H.M.S. *Centurion* were making plans for the demolition of the arsenal on leaving. It was decided to destroy everything, even the valuable guns and ammunition, because the fighting force would only be the same size as it was on the day of the relief, and it would have to protect a large convoy.

Nearly the whole of the admiral's party were needed to carry the stretchers, and so, although armed, were scarcely to be considered as fighting men on that occasion. As it became gradually dark more pickets were sent out, those on the railway embankment were strengthened, and as the whole of the wounded had crossed the river, the men began to make themselves as snug as possible for the night. It proved to be one of the most indescribably comfortless nights that it is possible to imagine. The sky was filled with a dull red glare from the immense numbers of burning houses; and this sight, with the monotonous sounds of howling curs, and distant gun fire, was so uncanny as to arouse all the superstition in one's mind.

In addition to this it was very damp and very cold, and as the men of the relieving column had not even their blankets with them, they suffered severely from the chill night air, and the miasma which rose in mists from the tainted river. The weirdness and the personal discomfort in fact were so great, that another possible reason for the restlessness which prevailed need hardly be taken into consideration. But there were very few there that night who did not expect that the Chinese would attack the camp in force before morning; and, indeed, it says but little for their general's military knowledge and initiative, that they should have let pass such a chance of attacking so comparatively small a force, which was in the open, and much hampered with wounded. Interesting as it would be to assign to them a reason for this and similar disastrous errors of judgment, it is outside the pretension of this little sketch to do so, though it would be most instructive to talk over this and other events of the campaign with an intelligent and truthful Chinese staff officer.

After this weird and restless night, at 2.30 a.m. the camp was roused, and the men were allowed to light their fires and brew their cocoa. There was no need for secrecy—the Chinese knew our position and intentions perfectly already, and the plain was soon alight with camp fires around which clustered the damp and shivering men. The arrangements as to the stretchers and carriers worked without a hitch, and at 3 a.m. the retirement commenced. Two officers belonging to H.M.S. *Centurion* stayed behind to start the fires, which it was hoped would entirely destroy the immense stores of ammunition and small arms, unfortunately but necessarily to be left.

This somewhat hazardous duty was successfully performed, and before dawn broke, the column saw huge clouds of smoke rising from the Arsenal, which had proved to be Seymour's salvation. Fires had been lit in five different places, and, from the apparent fierceness of the conflagration, it seemed as though its destruction must have been complete. We now know, however, that this was not quite the case; the heavy-gun ammunition and the field guns having escaped.

The march to Tientsin proved to be extremely tiring and tedious, the men of the admiral's force being naturally unable to keep up any great pace in their wretched condition, and with their comrades to carry. When the retirement started, most of the stretchers had a looted rifle or two beside the occupant, but very few of them ever got into Tientsin; the only thing of interest which was kept being one of the new captured Maxims, which has since been given to the officers and men of H.M.S. *Endymion*. Had fighting not been expected, of course the men of the relieving column would probably have dragged back some of the many useful guns from the arsenal; but under the circumstances it would have been inadvisable to add to the impediments of the already heavily encumbered force. The order of march was as follows: The advance guard of Russians, several hundred yards ahead of anyone, then another strong body of the relieving force, next came the long straggling line of stretchers with the sick and wounded, round which were the "reliefs" for the carriers, and last of all came the rear-guard, composed entirely of British and Americans.

The convoy moved, at a snail's pace, and it was seven o'clock before the bridge over the canal was reached. Here was evidence that the Russian sappers had been busy; for the bridge, which had only been roughly repaired on the previous crossing, now presented a thoroughly mended and passable appearance. From here, too, the settlement had been kept clear of any disturbing element by the Russians from Tientsin, so that all anxiety ceased at this point, and once more the allies were able to marvel at the extraordinary mixture of acuteness and imbecility which the Chinese leaders possessed in such a marked degree.

A shorter, and not so circuitous, route was taken on the return journey, and the badly battered station was reached about 11 a.m. Once again the force was within easy range of hostile guns, but so demoralised were the enemy at the allies' run of success, that they preferred to sulk behind their city walls, rather than renew the attack.

The enthusiasm among the Europeans was immense, and both columns were cheered to the echo; the excitement only abating as it became apparent that heavy losses had been suffered by the admiral's force. On the whole, the inhabitants had reason to be much more gay than sad, for during the last three days the garrison had been trebled, the place itself and Seymour's column, had both been rescued from exceptionally tight corners, and the Chinese had tasted the bitter humiliation which follows defeat. From another aspect the outlook was not so bright. Nearly all the admiral's men were in sore need of a prolonged rest, which was evident from the way the men collapsed, now that the strain was over.

Collapse is perhaps rather too strong a word; what is meant is that, whereas before, the men had scorned to utter complaint, they now felt it a duty to themselves to consult the doctor about the stomachic complaints from which they were nearly all suffering, and which had been brought on by precarious food supply, and the impure water which they had been compelled to drink. In addition to this, there were many more mouths to feed, a matter not to be lightly dismissed from mind at that time; and lastly, the Chinese would be able to concentrate their whole efforts on the capture of the settlements, without having two large forces employed; one in trying to keep out the relief force, the other in endeavouring to overwhelm the admiral.

Sir Edward Seymour was now the senior officer in Tientsin, and took over the command of the place. Affairs in Tientsin since the relief force had started, had not been altogether devoid of interest. The Commissioner of Customs had received a note from Sir Robert Hart to say that the Legations had been commanded to leave Pekin in twenty-our hours, and the letter was dated the 19th. This very naturally caused the greatest alarm about the persons of the Ministers and the Legation Guards; for after Seymour's experiences, everyone knew what the order meant.

If the command had been obeyed it simply spelt disaster, for once outside the city walls an army of 30,000 men would have slain them to a man! Another item of interest had been the arrival of a further detachment of the Chinese regiment. A fine, well set up, smart body of men, who seemed to have about as much objection to slaying their brother Chinese, as had the rest of the Allies, who were by this time getting rather bitterly disposed. A few shells were fired into the settlement towards evening, and it was noticed that the rifling of one of the heaviest was getting worn, for his projectiles used to turn over and over, making a most weird noise as they did so. But even these idiosyncrasies were insufficiently alarming to drive away sleep from the weary men of Seymour's column.

CHAPTER 7

Pei-Yang, Second Siege of Tientsin

The next day, June 27th, the Russian general decided that it was necessary to take the large eastern arsenal, about three and a half miles away, as it was known that it sheltered large bodies of the enemy, besides commanding the railway communication to Taku. Immediately the commander-in-chief heard of the project, he offered British assistance, but the Russian general replied that he felt able to take the place without aid, and so orders were given that the British would be granted a day's rest, after the arduous operations of the last few days. This was welcome news, and officers and men changed all their apparel, and made themselves comfortable preparatory, as they thought, to having a good day's sleep.

At 11 a.m., however, the "general assembly," was sounded, and orders were given that the utmost dispatch was necessary. In an incredibly short space of time, 500 of the naval brigade, two companies of the Wei-Hai-Wei regiment, and 50 American marines, under Major Waller, were under arms, and ready to proceed in any direction. It transpired that the Russians had been brought to a standstill by shell fire, while yet at extreme rifle range, and that their own fire had been rendered singularly ineffective by a very annoying mirage, which made it next to impossible to judge ranges at all accurately, or to discern any details at the point of attack.

When the force got under way, the diversity of uniforms caused much amusement. The marines were in their shirt sleeves, except those from the *Terrible*, who still donned their khaki, which they had worn in South Africa only a few months before. The bluejackets were in their ordinary blue 'jumpers,' but a great many of the officers had indulged in the luxury of a clean white duck uniform, which of course they had no time to change; so they perforce had to remain by far and away the most conspicuous objects on the fields. On their way, the force passed the 12-pr. from the *Terrible*, which had been ineffectively shelling the position at 5000 yards' range, and was waiting for more ammunition. This arrived just as they passed, and the gun began to drop shells with great accuracy of the powder manufactory, and other storehouses and workshops.

Advancing under cover of the line, which connected the arsenal with the railway, the reinforcing column reached a point where the cover ceased, and it became necessary to deploy under fire. On the British right lay long lines of white-coated Russians, with three maxims and a battery, and it was thought from their distance to the arsenal—some 3,000 yards—that they had delivered an attack, but had been beaten off. This proved not to have been the case. They had merely exceeded even their usual slowness in the attack, and had fired volleys steadily for some time at an object, the detail of which, as I have said, was invisible. Eventually, finding that the Chinese meant to stay, their commanding officer had sent in for reinforcements.

As they were all under some sort of cover, and our men were obliged to lie down in the open on a perfectly flat plain, it wasn't long before the Chinese turned their undivided attention to the British, and subjected them to a well-directed shrapnel fire from two field guns mounted in the south-west corner of their position.

After waiting for ten minutes, a message was sent to the Russian general that the British wished to advance to within effective range. The reply to this was to the effect that the advance would begin in five minutes. Ten minutes passed, but no advance, so another message was sent saying that the British would advance alone, if the Russians did not move forward in ten minutes' time. The same reply as before was received; but as no movement became visible for a quarter of an hour, and several men had been hit by shrapnel bullets, the "advance" was sounded and the line swung forward. Before the ground of the bugle had died away, there was a tremendous explosion in the arsenal, caused either by the *Terrible's* 12-pr., which was now making beautiful shooting, or by the Chinese themselves. Our gun had also knocked out a small quick-firer, which had greatly harassed the Russians, and had temporarily silenced one of the two guns, which were playing on the left of the advance.

It was not long before the enemy understood that the British were trying to envelop their extreme rights which would be one of their lines of retreat, and the first signs of discovery were the almost entire cessation of firing on their left, and a corresponding on the British line of advance, which, however, gradually became normal as they got nearer and nearer.

The loss in the Chinese trenches was probably inconsiderable, for but little firing was indulged in; the trenches afforded excellent cover, and of course the mirage was another great source of protection. The advance was a quick one, and it was with difficulty that the men could be restrained from charging when the fire began to grow hot, and casualties to take place. When the fighting line was within 300 yards of the walls, bayonets were fixed and the "charge" was sounded. This proved too much for the enemy, who could be plainly seen to be leaving the walls in twos and threes, and who appeared to be all making for the right of their position.

Unfortunately for them, the marines had pushed far enough forward to inflict heavy loss on them as they ran, and the Chinese, who at first attempted to retain some kind of order in their retreat, were compelled to scatter, and became a disorganized mob. At this juncture some 4000 Boxers attacked the left of the British line in the rear, and were not noticed until they were within a quarter of a mile. It was lucky they had not come on before, for the line had had their hands quite full with the task of turning the enemy out of his position in front, and any confusion must have greatly helped the enemy in their retreat, even if it had not resulted in the attack being rolled back.

As it was, the Chinese regiment, who were in support, coolly turned about, and drove them back handsomely, by a well directed fire which inflicted some loss. The only regrettable incident in this little diversion was the slaying and dismemberment of two wounded marines, who in some unaccountable manner had been missed by the stretcher parties and left in the rear, right in the path of the Boxers, into whose hands they fell. That they had made a fight for it, was evident by the dead bodies of two Boxers, one of whom had been shot, and the other bayoneted.

All that was left of these poor fellows was interred on the spot. Once inside the ramparts, all opposition ceased, and the only casualty which occurred there, was to a bluejacket, who was killed by some lurking Chinaman, who fired through a window of a hut at a range of about two yards. The man died instantly, but his death was avenged by his slayer being bayoneted by a couple of bluejackets, who rushed into the house and brought out his dead body.

So eager were the last party of the enemy to escape from the Russians, who by this time had entered on the other side, that they rushed madly across the front of a strong party of British, whom they did not observe until too late. Many were slain. As usual the want of cavalry was severely felt, and it was a heartbreaking scene to see the masses of fugitives, numbering in all about four thousand, streaming across the plain in a hopeless rout, without being able to launch a few squadrons of lancers at them to complete their discomfiture. It was hopeless to follow them with infantry alone, and the men had to content themselves with lining the deserted walls, and pouring in a hot fire until they realised that the Chinese were out of range. Of course the Russians claimed the lion's share, and promptly took the place into their possession, and began to loot it thoroughly.

In the buildings of the naval college were some magnificent astronomical instruments, besides models, and a splendid library of standard works, all in English, but to the ignorant Russian soldiery they had no monetary value, and so too often their fate was to be bayoneted, or hammered to pieces by the butts of their rifles.

The British force withdrew as soon as the enemy were out of sight, and it had become evident that the allies were in undisputed possession of the arsenal; and the Russians were left in sole command, with the proviso that the Union Jack should be kept flying as long as the place was in European hands.

The day's operations had been very important, for besides the immense moral effect it must have had on the enemy, who had been turned out of a good strategic and defensive position, it practically made the Russian and German camps on that side of the river immune from attack. The moral effect was so great, moreover, that for two days the enemy appeared to be entirely cowed, and no further operations, except the usual desultory bombardment, were indulged in by either side.

The allies took advantage of the rest, and sent down most of the sick and wounded of Seymour's column to be attended to at the fleet. On arriving there, they were immediately sent down to Wei-Hai-Wei, where there were better arrangements for their comfort. Reinforcements arrived in the shape of a regiment of Japanese infantry, and on the 29th the men from H.M.S. *Alacrity* rejoined their ship. On the 30th too, the station again became the scene of a desperate struggle culminating in another Chinese reverse.

The enemy's guns commanding this important position were extremely well placed. The guns themselves were completely hidden, but the gunners from their emplacements could just see the roofs of the station buildings, of which they had the range so accurately that they repeatedly made the place too warm for the Allies' infantry, who perforce had to take to trenches in the open.

Up to this time, however, the Chinese had made no attempt to cut the river communications, and guns and troops were steadily being landed at Taku and sent up to the front by tugs and lighters. On the 30th the Governor-General of Port Arthur arrived, in the person of Vice-Admiral Alexieff, so that Tientsin was beginning to reach the unenviable state of having so many commanding officers of the same rank, that it was always uncertain how the various necessary dispositions of one force would be received by the others; in fact it was a case of the proverbial "*too many cooks, etc.*"

About this time, the enemy received large reinforcements, matters looked very serious again, and martial law was proclaimed.

On July 2nd, the British headquarter barracks *Barfleur* had an extremely narrow escape from fire. The 'godown' next door caught alight in some unaccountable manner, and burned with the utmost fury, causing great anxiety for the safety of the food and ammunition in the barracks.

It was a miserably wet day, and the men could procure practically no appliances to get it under, but although the barrack roof and shutters caught fire and smouldered, the excellent work done by all hands saved the building, and in three or four hours the 'godown' burnt itself out. The flames had not been in progress for ten minutes before it became quite evident what were the contents of the house; thick streams of boiling sugar poured out of the windows, doors, and every crevice in the wall, until at last the bund in front of the barracks, and the spacious yard behind, were veritable ponds of molasses, about a foot deep. An attempt was made to clear up the mess made by the still warm mixture, but it proved abortive, so much so that an unwary company of little Japs got literally stuck in it, looking for all the world like so many flies on a fly-paper. In the evening Midshipman Donaldson died of his wounds, two in number, which he received in his first engagement. He had been shot in the neck, and again through the right lung, the latter proving fatal at the commencement of the rainy season, which had been expected for a week or so.

On the 3rd, matters took a turn for the worse, and the enemy became more pressing in their attacks, and more steady in their bombardment. The fighting at the station was constant and severe, and had it not been for the reinforcements, it looked as if the defence must have been worn down under the incessant strain. The women and children all went down to Taku by command of Admiral Seymour, except a few who elected to continue their work of mercy in the hospitals, and who were allowed to remain.

On the night of the 4th, a strong body of the enemy arrived from the southward, and proceeded to burn the two magnificent country houses out by the racecourse, which, needless to say, were owned by Europeans, but which had been untouched as yet. The same force formed a camp in the racecourse,—which, with its surroundings, was a very strong natural position,—and continued to harass the concessions from it with artillery. The enemy also closed in on the settlement with their other guns to such an extent, that a determined effort was made on Friday to dislodge some of them.

The most annoying gun of all was a 6-pr. which was mounted within 500 yards of the French settlement, but whose exact position was not clear; so a reconnoitring party was sent out to discover its whereabouts, the troops being two companies of bluejackets from H.M.S. *Barfleur*, part of the Wei-Hai-Wei regiment, and some Americans who were kept in reserve. The movement was successful, and the enemy unmasked their position, a brisk rifle fire being maintained for about an hour, when, having discovered the enemy's strength, numbers, and dispositions, the Europeans retired without loss.

In the afternoon, the native city was subjected to a concentrated fire from every gun that the Allies possessed, and surmising that the Chinese would be paying more attention to the bombardment than to the French settlement, it was decided that the gun which had been located in the morning should be attacked in the afternoon, when the bombardment was at its height. At one o'clock, fire was opened on the city from twenty-five guns. Thirteen of these were British: five 12-pr. from the *Terrible*; four 7-pr. M.L. (an Indian mountain battery); two 14-pr. Krupps captured from the enemy at the taking of Taku forts; one 6-pr. Q.F. naval gun; and one 9-pr. M.L., also naval.

Six of the others were Japanese, and the remaining six were French. The enemy made a spirited reply to the bombardment, and their artillerists made some excellent practice, hitting the sand bags around the naval guns several times. The 6-pr. had its back-sight shot away, and a pickaxe lying in the gunpit was also destroyed. The casualties, considering everything, were ridiculously small, and although the enemy's fuses were accurately set, and the number of blind shell but few, yet the fire proved singularly ineffective.

The effect of the Allies' fire, on the contrary, was soon visible. The *pagodas* dotted all over the city, which were used by the Chinese as look-out towers, crumbling up and falling in, burning themselves, and setting light to other buildings, was indeed a sharp reminder of the past three weeks, when the Allies had been impotent to reply. The city, like all other Chinese towns, was densely built, and thickly populated; and under the fire, which lasted for four hours, many of the inhabitants must have lost their lives. One very sad incident occurred at the height of the artillery duel. The shells used by the captured Chinese guns were of a variety known as ringed shell, and were of an excessively sensitive nature. To prevent accidents, while loading they had a plug in the head of each, which acted as a safety arrangement until the weapon was fired.

In some way this had become displaced in one of them, and on placing it in the breech it exploded, blowing one of the marine gunner's arms off, and wounding several others. The two guns were not afterwards employed; they are now filling the position of trophies at Whale Island—the Naval School of Gunnery near Portsmouth. About half-past two, another move was made in the direction of the object of the morning's reconnaissance; the composition of the force being the same, with the addition of a 9-pr. gun for which it was hoped to find a position, whence the enemy's gun could be silenced, before starting the attack. Unfortunately the Chinese had evidently anticipated some movement of the kind, for they had reinforced their position strongly, and fighting commenced before the attacking force had got 300 yards away from the French settlement.

It soon became evident that a hopeless task lay before them; the position for their gun, which had been selected carefully in the morning, was now full of the enemy, and the houses in their front were positively teeming with Imperial troops who kept up a hot fire on anything in the shape of a hat, boot, or rifle that was visible. A flanking movement was impossible because of the very limited space in which they fought, and for the same reason only a very small number of the troops engaged could come into action. This did not apply to the enemy, because the Allies were in reality attacking the vertex of a triangle, whereas the Chinese were defending the base.

The Wei-Hai-Wei regiment was in the fighting line, and fought most doggedly for some time, but finding it impracticable to advance, and the casualties becoming rather heavy, the whole force fell back on the French barricade, their rear protected by the two companies of seamen from the *Barfleur*, who retired by sections, firing as they went, until the whole force moved into safety. It was just before the retirement commenced that the officer in command of the fighting line (Major Bruce) was severely wounded, at the same moment that Midshipman Esdaile received two wounds which shortly proved fatal.

The Chinese were so unaccustomed to seeing the backs of the Allies, that they screwed up enough courage to commence a charge which was never finished, because those in rear saw the prompt death which was meted out to the first of their comrades who broke cover.

On reaching the barricade, the men took shelter, and waited for a counter attack. There were very angry men behind the barrier of merchandise that afternoon; their anger was expressed by their rather curious words; they talked about having to retire, in language one does not use in conversation with friends, and but little of which would be found in any dictionary. They got slightly better humoured when some of the officers, who were equally worried, and who only expressed their annoyance in slightly milder terms, began to talk about the bayonet; but they relapsed into their usual excellent self-control, when this proposal was negative, as being too desperate a remedy to employ for the mere gratification of the men's passions. The barricade was manned, and all Chinamen who showed themselves became the objects of much attention.

After waiting for some time, two Boxers, armed only with swords, ran round a corner about 100 yards away, and appeared to be endeavouring to urge the Imperial troops to charge. Their instant fate, however, must have had a diametrically opposite effect!

When everything became quiet, the force marched back to barracks, very sick at the non-success of their venture. However, the gun did not again fire from this position, so it may be supposed that the Allies had succeeded in frightening the enemy pretty badly, even if they did not inflict any very great loss upon them.

The next two days were spent in mounting two 4-in. guns which arrived from the *Algerine* and *Phoenix*, while the Chinese endeavoured to drive the Allies' guns off the mud wall near the wool-mill. Although shelled from five different places, the guns were excellently served, and succeeded in silencing three of the hostile guns which had advanced to within but little more than 2000 yards' range.

On the 8th poor young Esdaile was buried, and laid close to Donaldson, the other midshipman who had died from wounds a few days previously—whose greatest friend he had been. The two had been inseparable in life, and by some fatal decree it was ordained that death should claim them alone, out of all the midshipmen landed, many of whom were more or less severely wounded.

The cemetery was but 200 yards from the gas-works, and during the funeral service, the Chinese were most persistent in trying to destroy the light supply. Luckily, they could not see the gasometers, and so had to fire by guess-work; and although the houses and walls in their immediate vicinity suffered heavily, the gas-works themselves were untouched.

Now for the first time it was noticed that the enemy were threatening the river, and as the importance of keeping this only means of communication open was vital, the Japanese general proposed to intercept the movement, drive the enemy back, and if possible let the day's work culminate in the capture of the Hi-Kuan-Su arsenal, which it will be remembered was a small arsenal about a mile and a half to the westward.

Accordingly, at half-past two on the morning of the 9th, a force of 2200 men, comprising Japs, British, and Russians, left by the Taku gates to endeavour to surprise the enemy in his advanced positions.

At about four o'clock the first shots were fired a mile before the racecourse was reached, and in a few minutes the engagement became general. After a brief struggle the Japs shelled them out of their trenches, and driving them back across the plain, managed to get into them with their cavalry, who, despite the paucity of their numbers, charged through and through the fugitives, and slew some 240.

Much surprise and chagrin were felt at the total disappearance, for a time, of the enemy's guns, which had been located the evening before, but after a brilliant bayonet charge in a village—in which not a shot was fired, but 150 Chinamen lost their lives—the guns were discovered, half hidden under some rubbish.

The next thing to be done was to change front to the right, and attack the arsenal, which was only about three-quarters of a mile distant. It was first subjected to a heavy shell fire from the Japanese and Indian artillery, who burst clouds of shrapnel all over its face, and who were in turn shelled by two very small, but very diligent, quick-firing field guns. The latter had bad luck, for although they kept up an exceedingly rapid and very accurate fire, the damage done to the Allies was practically *nil*. The shells appeared to be too small to do any considerable damage, even if exactly placed, and became, as the day went on, contemptible as far as danger went, though admirable in their pertinacity and the skill with which they fled to their harmless destination.

When the way had been prepared by the artillery, the advance commenced, the British and Japanese making the frontal, the Americans a flank attack. The resistance was trifling, and the arsenal was taken possession of at about ten o'clock. From the cover of the walls the enemy were harassed in their retreat by rifle and gun fire, but it is improbable that their losses were at all heavy. It was at first proposed to garrison the place, but eventually it was decided to abandon it, for many reasons.

Unfortunately, that part which faced the native city was not defended by any wall, or entrenched in any way, and as the distance was but about 2000 yards, it was open to long-range rifle fire which would soon have made it untenable, to say nothing of the enemy's artillery, which could have speedily demolished every building.

Then again, there would have been the communications to keep open, which, although it would have been a comparatively easy task, was imposing needless work on the troops; consequently, after everything of military worth had been destroyed, the force began their return journey. They were assiduously shelled from the precincts of the city, and fired upon by concealed snipers for the whole distance, and unfortunately lost several men.

Soon after this, on the arrival of further reinforcements, it was rumoured that plans were being matured, by the carrying out of which the native city should be stormed and occupied.

Accordingly, no one was much surprised when, two nights later, orders were given to the naval brigade to be ready to march out with the Russians at 2 a.m. The British, Japanese, and Americans were to attack the southern gate, while the French and Russians were to have operated on the other bank of the river. The men were called at a quarter past one, and, as the old adage that "*an Englishman fights best on a full belly*" is still very true, they were fed preparatory to departure.

Unfortunately the message to start never came: instead came a Russian who "was very sorry, but would everyone go to bed again, as somehow or other their sappers hadn't been able to prepare the way."

As one of the officers remarked:

This was disquieting news, for to turn in at 2 a.m. with one's belly full of boiling porridge, is not half such fun as scrapping with Chinamen, nor is it so healthy.

Be that as it may, the haunting nightmare, which it may safely be inferred visited that officer, was not allowed to have a free hand in the headquarter barracks that morning, for suddenly the enemy opened on the settlement with a terrific shell fire, which capsized one of the chimneys over the officer's sleeping room, and filled the whole place with dust and smoke. One shell burst in the men's quarters, and by the extraordinary fatalism which pursued the *Centurion's* men throughout the operations, the only man hit belonged to that ship. He, poor fellow, was the only *Centurion* man in barracks.

Even this alarm was not the last, for at four o'clock a marine, breathless and capless, rushed in, and reported that the station was being attacked by a large force, who were fighting with more than their ordinary bravery, and who were gradually enveloping the position. B company *Barfleurs*, and the company of the Hong-Kong regiment were immediately despatched to reinforce the defenders, who consisted of the *Terrible's* marines and some Frenchmen, whose ammunition was practically exhausted. The Pathans crossed the river and advanced by a somewhat circuitous route along the railway line, on to which all the empty trucks had been shunted from the station, and which afforded good cover.

On this occasion, however, the trucks were tenanted, and a sergeant had just time to yell "Chinese in the trucks!" when he was shot dead, and a heavy fire was opened on to the remainder of the company. Without a moment's hesitation the Indians went in with the bayonet, and within a minute or two this part of the enemy were in full retreat. B company moved up by a more direct path, being greeted, while crossing the river, by a shrapnel shell which burst right above the company, but, marvellously enough, hit no one.

On arriving at the station, matters were found to be even worse than the man had said. Some of the enemy were ensconced behind a bank some 30 yards to the front, and their fixed bayonets could be seen as they moved to and fro, evidently summoning up courage for a charge, in the event of which the little garrison would only have escaped annihilation by a miracle. But little firing was going on, our men husbanding their last nine rounds each for the final rush, and the enemy evidently not liking to expose their valuable carcases to take aim. Certainly the enemy in the rear had been keeping up a hot, but comparatively innocuous fire, whilst those in front occasionally "eased off" without taking any aim at all; perhaps invoking Joss to find a satisfactory resting place for their bullets.

On the arrival of reinforcements, however, the Chinese finally made up their minds that it wasn't good enough, and at once commenced to retire. As it was now getting light, and they had 100 yards of open ground to traverse, they lost heavily from the deliberate and accurate fire which burst out with renewed vigour from the station, and the open was quickly strewn with more of war's victims. The retreat was not continued very far, and on reaching the excellent cover afforded by the graves, already mentioned, they resumed a galling rifle fire before again withdrawing. Immediately they had retired, their artillery opened fire, and the Allies had again to leave the locomotive shed, the walls and roof of which were by this time absolutely pulverized; and it would be rash on the part of any one to hazard an estimate of the number of shell marks which it bore. Very soon, however, the Japs and Russians sent detachments of men to the threatened point, and all fear of the success of the Chinese attack was at an end.

Towards eight o'clock the enemy planted banners on two of the biggest mounds as a sign of defiance, but finding that they attracted our fire, they soon hauled them down and began to retire sullenly under cover of a heavy shelling from our guns. With the exception of the first fight at the station, this, which proved to be the last, was the most severe. Up to date the enemy's tactics had been childish in the extreme, and each previous attack had been heralded by a terrific storm of rifle fire. On this occasion, however, they had presumably got into position to resist the projected Russian attack of the night before, and, finding themselves so close to the coveted station, attacked it vigorously on ascertaining that the movement had fallen through. This is of course merely conjecture, but there is much to be said for such a line of argument, for their knowledge of every move, and indeed every plan, inside the settlement, throughout both sieges, was little short of marvellous.

The 11th was passed amidst a storm of shells from both sides, the 4-in. gun, mounted out towards Pei-Yang arsenal, having a two hours' duel with four guns mounted close to the banks of the canal at a range of 4000 yards. Three of the four were silenced, but the fourth gave as good as it took till the very end, when the cessation of fire was mutual. The next day was the exact opposite of its predecessor, there was no early morning fighting, and even shelling did not begin until the evening. It was a Heaven-sent rest, for much remained to be done in the way of fatigue work and gun mounting, to prepare for the morrow, which was the day chosen to assume the offensive and attack the native city.

A German 6-in. gun arrived, but was not mounted, and although carpenters were busy constructing a mounting for the 4.7-in. which arrived on the 11th, and the engineers made an emplacement and magazine for it, the work could not be finished in time to take part in the great effort of the morrow, and was abandoned. Admiral Seymour and the remainder of his brigade went down to Taku by river in the afternoon, thereby just missing the hardest battle in the naval brigade's experience, and an operation which proved to be the most important—in fact the turning-point of the whole campaign. Their departure was the last thing of importance which took place in the period 27th June to 12th July, between which dates began and ended the second siege of Tientsin.

CHAPTER 8

Capture of Tientsin Native City

Two o'clock on the morning of July 13th saw bodies of men, totalling rather more than 6000, moving quietly to their appointed rendezvous; from which they were to set out to fight what proved to be the fiercest battle of the war, a battle against heavy odds, and one in which every advantage lay with the opposing forces. The object in view was the capture of the native city, without which the advance to Pekin might be indefinitely delayed, and which was, equally with the capture of the Taku Forts, the most important operation of the many which finally resulted in the relief of the Legations. The native city itself, besides being surrounded by a high and solid wall which was impervious to the attacks of the Allies' light artillery, was also the most important city in the north of China, with the single exception of Pekin.

It was the centre of the huge fur trade, and in fact was the outlet to 90 *per cent*, of the entire trade of two provinces. The population was about a million souls, and it was garrisoned by regular troops to the computed number of 12,000, with another 10,000 Boxers as armed auxiliaries. The latter had nearly all got rifles of types from the newest Mannlichers to old single-loading Mausers, with which, even if they were not adepts in the art of rifle shooting, they at least kept up an astonishingly heavy fusillade. They appeared to labour under some misapprehension about the use of sights, which they seemed to believe denoted the muzzle velocity of the projectile, rather than the number of yards at which it was desired to kill a foreign devil. Thus, seeing a man say about 200 yards away, they thought that if they put up their sights to about 1800 yards, they stood more chance of hurting him than they would do if content with the proper range.

Unfortunately this did not apply to the Regulars, who on this

Gun and ensign captured at Tientsin

occasion, urged on by threats and bribes, used their weapons more effectively than was looked for, judging by their past behaviour. Even before the troops had started the enemy had somehow or other got the news, and shells began to fall pretty frequently in the German concession, which was the quarter fixed for the gathering of the British, Japanese, Americans, and French. The representatives of these powers were entrusted with the attack on the south gate of the city, after they had driven back the enemy from the Hi-Kuan-Su arsenal, which was already occupied again by the Chinese.

The Russians and Germans were told to capture all the batteries and forts on the other side of the river, and then to catch the enemy as he retreated from the north gate and fled, as every one confidently expected he would, along the river bank to Hsi-Ku arsenal, the scene of Seymour's relief, which had also been re-occupied by Ma's men. To the superstitious the day appeared to be an unhappily chosen one, for not only was it the thirteenth of the month, but it laboured under the somewhat grave disadvantage of being a Friday, two misfortunes upon which an officer was flippant enough to pass some facetious remarks, as the naval brigade headed the British force out of the Taku gate.

The total number of men engaged was about 5000, British 710, Japanese 1500, French 900, Austrians 45, and Americans 900, who were on the south-west side of the river, the Russian and German contingent being on the north-east. The first line of advance assumed the form of a sweep, and took the force clear of the enemy's artillery only loss, for here Captain Lloyd of the Marines was mortally wounded in the throat, while yet relating his experiences of the Seymour column. Almost his last words were to the effect that, having come safely through that trying time, he feared not for his safety then. The conduct and the courage of the men were splendid.

They showed the utmost confidence that the order which regulated them to he on the fire-swept plain, and prevented them from gaining the shelter of the arsenal walls, only some two or three hundred yards in front, was only given, that something more important to the main issue should first take place before their work began. At last the tension was removed, the order to advance was given, and with what feelings of relief the men rose, formed into line, and marched coolly up to the walls, can be better imagined than described. Only two men were lost whilst in the erect position, whereas the small British naval force alone, on rising, left one officer dead and some twenty wounded men in the doctor's hands. Naturally the interval had not passed without incidents occurring which in some measure affected the result of the battle. The first was a terrific explosion on the other side of the city, which proved to have been caused by the demolition of a dynamite store, either by British guns or Russian bullets.

The effects of the explosion were somewhat curious; a squadron of Cossacks were dismounted, and it was said that the Russian general was himself slightly injured by the falling debris. Many windows in the settlement were broken at a distance of two miles, and where the Naval Brigade were lying in their previously described position, the vibration was extraordinary, at a distance of about three and a half miles. A thin column of white smoke rose perpendicularly in the still air, and gradually flattened out into a mushroom-like pall; perchance the only pall to the coffins of several of the enemy.

Another noticeable event was a minor explosion on the south side of the city, occasioned by a shell from the 12-pr. on the mud wall. It burst in a small-arm magazine, and caused an outbreak which finally developed into a serious fire, sounding for all the world like hundreds of crackers going off, as the fire reached box after box of ammunition. One thing was noticeable during that inactive half hour, in which one had nothing to do but think; it was the manner in which the wounded men behaved on receiving their bullet. What a lot some actors might learn if they only would take the risk of being eye-witnesses!

There would be less of the tragic fall on to one's back, and less still of the fixed stare at the drop scenery. In reality, it is only the slightly wounded who betray any emotion whatever, and this is nearly all of a facial type, their utterances are usually not fit for publication. The more seriously wounded seem to be numbed, and their phlegm seems wonderful in such circumstances; no whining, no apparent excitement, a very common remark with bluejackets being "'ave got! get a stretcher. Bill"—practical if callous. Those who figure in the day's casualty list as mortally wounded, if speech remain to them, generally seem to have had some premonition of the coming disaster,—they are "fey." Their feelings are expressed by "I felt it coming," or "Them —— have got me at last," and so on.

When the brigade reached the arsenal, it was seen that the Japanese were pressing an attack in skirmishing order on the left front, the Americans were discovered to be about to start to the right front in force, while the straight and exposed road joining the arsenal with the south gate of the city, was held by a mixed force of French and Japanese numbering in all about a hundred, who had pushed up to within

600 yards of the gate, in order to take advantage of the cover afforded by some half-dozen huts. This small body had two guns with them, but these speedily became inoperative through lack of ammunition, and the extreme danger, which lay in making an attempt to bring a further supply from the rear, rendered them useless for the remainder of the day.

By half-past nine, the day had grown unpleasantly hot, and the men of the British contingent contrived to snatch a few minutes' rest under the shadow of the mud wall, which proved to be an efficient sunshade, as well as a valuable shield. The furious musketry and artillery duel continued without cessation, and it seemed likely that the Japanese and Americans, devoid of all cover as they were, might be compelled to retire. Certain it is, that any further advance seemed fraught with such dangers that it was improbable the city would fall during the daytime. One may, therefore, judge of the surprise caused by a message to General Fukushima, that some Japanese troops had already gained a footing inside the walls.

At the time it struck every one as being too improbable to be correct, but immediate action was necessary to support any body of men who might have won their way in, and on the earnest desire of the Naval Brigade's commander to be given the post, the order was given that two companies of marines, and a company of bluejackets, should advance down the central road straight to the gate, and that another company of bluejackets should be sent to the aid of the Americans, who appeared to have suffered a serious check in their advance on the S.E. corner of the wall, and on the suburbs in their immediate front. With the first-named detachments went a half company of the Chinese regiment, who seemed every whit as keen on the chance of some desperate street fighting as the sailors.

The whole body marched through the captured arsenal and found, on the other side, a Japanese field battery, pounding away for all it was worth, at the south gate, receiving in return a heavy shell fire, and an equally heavy, but ill-directed rifle fire. This of course dashed the story, that the gate had fallen, to the ground, and on leaving the friendly cover of the houses, it became apparent that the party to be reinforced would not be reached without an advance, in which the elements of excitement and danger were not lacking, and in which the latter largely predominated. There were some 1200 yards to be covered, the ground to be crossed consisting of a straight, flat road about 15 yards wide, with canals on each side of it; at the other end, at a range of about 1900 yards, were 3000 riflemen with several guns, the whole in comparative safety; and the only opportunity for a spell of rest offered itself in the shape of two small huts about half way.

The marines led in single file at the double, and the other companies taking the movement up, there was soon a long khaki and blue snake on the road, to serve as a target for the Chinamen. Scarcely had the rear of the line left cover, when the comparatively peaceful road became dotted with bullets, which, with the splashes in the adjacent canals, went to make the onlooker hold his breath with anxiety to see how long the fire would be in taking effect. It was not long, first one, and then two others, falling forward; but on the whole the casualties were surprisingly light during the first half of the journey. The looked-for rest at the halfway hut, which had held forth such an alluring prospect, turned out to be most uncomfortable, as the spot was semi-enfiladed from a walled prison on the left, and two more casualties took place. About three minutes saw the men again advancing, and as they emerged from the little stopping place, a withering fire came from the suburbs, the prison, and innumerable loopholes in the top of the city wall.

The Chinese must have been considerably upset at the general trend of events, for they missed an opportunity such as but seldom falls to the lot of any number of snugly entrenched troops. Every man should have been hit, so great was the expenditure of ammunition; but although the casualties were rather more numerous—three men being killed, and an officer and a dozen or so others wounded,—on the whole the force again escaped lightly. It was during the second advance that Midshipman Guy of the *Barfleur* gained his V.C. for bandaging a wounded man under this heavy fire, and eventually carrying him back to shelter, where unfortunately his wounds proved fatal. Everything comes to an end, and at last the houses were reached. These proved to be big enough to shelter the whole force, as well as the mixed detachments already there; the total number would be about 300, comprising Japanese, French, Austrians, marines, bluejackets, and some of the Chinese regiment.

So crowded were the men at first, that those who were not energetic enough to explore for themselves, had to lie out in the rear of the centre house, a position which was open to fire from two sides; and it was not until a Frenchman and one of the Chinese regiment had been killed, that some of them began to look about them, and to make the most of the ample cover that there was. In order to eliminate the objectionably long term "the Author," and to facilitate the flow of incident, I, who happened to be one of the midshipmen with the party, propose to take up the thread of the narrative:—

The wounded with us suffered frightfully, being without bandages and also without water, this latter being so near and yet so very far, for two men who crawled down to the muddy canals to fill water bottles were both shot in the head; and in addition to our other troubles, a field gun made our position its objective, before we had been there an hour. Unlike the majority of gunners who served the Chinese artillery, the No. 1 of this gun made the most execrable shooting, and the first ten shells flew all more or less wide of the mark. The eleventh, however, entered the roof of one of the houses and burst in the little central courtyard, which luckily was untenanted. I have still in my possession the base and fuse of this shell, which so nearly levied toll on the crowded men just on the other side of the four enclosing walls.

Half a minute passed, and we were still waiting for the twelfth, when our 12-pr., a mile and a quarter away, woke up, and caused the retirement of the tormenter. But for this relief at the eleventh hour, there can be no doubt that our position would have shortly become untenable. For the next few hours we laboured to put the position in a state of defence, but the fire became so hot, if even as much as an arm were shown, that it was impracticable to get much done. A Frenchman and a marine who were, contrary to orders, sniping from an improvised loophole, both got hit, the former fatally.

A very plucky exhibition of despatch-carrying was shown by three Japanese mounted orderlies, who were trying to reach the officer in command of the small Japanese detachment who shared our quarters, or to be more accurate, whose quarters we shared. They had come from the arsenal, and had reached the halfway hut safely. Here they dismounted, and one remounting, galloped towards us lying low in his saddle. He had barely got 50 yards when horse and man were rolled over lifeless. The second also rode to his death, but without a moment's hesitation the third took his horse by the bridle, and leading it, managed to reach us safely amidst great excitement, only to lose his horse, which took fright at some bullet graze and galloped back whence they had come, pursued by a shower of bullets.

About the same time as this, another incident occurred with even more fatal results to the parties concerned. Lieutenant Oliphant, with two of the Chinese regiment and two mules, had already twice taken ammunition to the hard-pressed Americans, and he once more essayed the same task. In less than half-a-minute from the time of his leaving cover, men, mules, and ammunition lay in a heap on the ground, inert and lifeless. There is an adage which has it that "it *The third time does.*" It did!

The Americans for their part had suffered heavily, and for some reason, perhaps the comparative laxity of discipline which obtains in their service, they were beginning to show loss of morale, an adjunct of vital importance to troops in adverse circumstances. One man was heard to say "Guess I don't mind scrapping of a kind, but may I go back and scrap in the Philippines for the rest of my mortal life, rather than any more of this." He was so evidently in earnest that it was rather laughable, and one of the petty officers belonging to the company of bluejackets who had been sent to their support, took occasion to assure him that he would get used to it like himself, who had had that sort of amusement nearly every meal-time for four weeks!

Undoubtedly their share of the fight had been an arduous one. They had to advance over difficult open ground, they had lost five officers, and though it appeared that they might have cleared the villages in their front with a little dash, it would perhaps have been a hazardous operation to undertake, considering their loss in men and morale. Failing an advance, there was nothing for them to do but hang on to their position until darkness, in order to prevent our centre from being enveloped by troops from the enemy's left; to retire by daylight was, besides being bad strategy, demoralising and extremely dangerous. Thus this weary day dragged on, until at four o'clock in the afternoon, there seemed to be even less chance of getting into the city than had been the case at ten o'clock in the morning.

At four o'clock, as no communication or further orders had been received either from General Dorward or Captain Burke, I was sent back with a note to each of them, asking for instructions in the one, and for a doctor—whom I met on the way—and food, water, stretchers, etc., in the other. My appearance was of course the signal for a furious but badly aimed fusillade, which continued until I had reached the arsenal, which I did after a most exciting run. I had only left our position about five yards when a bullet grazed my hand and took the skin off two of my knuckles, and I'll bet I beat all records for the 100 yards. On my way, after this, a Frenchman passed me, bent on a similar errand in the opposite direction. He, poor fellow, when within 5 yards of me, fell with a splash into one of the canals.

There was just time to glance at him before hurrying onwards, the result of the investigation being more flattering to Chinese marksmanship than one would have imagined, his wounds numbering two, either of which would have been sufficient to kill him. I had reason to feel sorry for the poor chap, because perhaps one had been meant for me! In the arsenal, preparations were being made for the night, and it was not without some seeking that the General was found, returning from personally placing the Royal Welsh Fusiliers in an excellent position for repulsing any attack on the left flank. In the rear were three thousand of the enemy's infantry, and some cavalry and guns; with these the Japanese cavalry were in touch, but their presence in the vicinity necessitated very careful dispositions being made.

Two companies of sailors were sent to occupy some few houses, in reality a tiny village, commanding the road, the only possible line of approach for cavalry, and their absence from the arsenal, which was to all intents our base, created a great scarcity of men there. This was however remedied by the return, under cover of darkness, of the Americans and the company of our sailors. Our wounded were also sent back to safety, and a cartful of water and food, which returned with me to our position on the road, served the double purpose of conveying provender in the outward trip, and being a comfortable conveyance for them on the homeward one.

The Allies' arrangements were, that the main force of Japanese should press their attack right home on to the suburbs underneath the walls, and should occupy them, until plans had been completed to blow open the south gate, which it was proposed to do at four in the morning; also that our mixed force should maintain its position until the explosion was heard, when we were to immediately rush forward straight for the gate, which, together with the south wall, we had to occupy. We, in turn, were going to be relieved by the Americans and the other troops, who were all going to hurry up at the given signal. The utmost confidence prevailed, and after everyone had partaken of some food and drink, it was felt on all hands that a great success awaited us on the morrow.

Sentries were posted, positions assigned to the various contingents in case of a sortie, and the men lay down to get as much rest as possible. According to custom, a heavy fire was maintained by the Chinese all night long, but, with two exceptions, the night passed quietly. One was the wounding of a marine by a chance bullet, the other was caused by a party of Frenchmen who, on it commencing to rain, tried to crowd into a hut which was being used by some of our officers. On being cleared out they were most indignant, seeming to think that six feet, by ten feet, by six feet was ample accommodation for about thirty human beings, and they assured us that they were "*bons camarades!*" Perhaps they were, but, with the exception of a couple, they had to find shelter elsewhere.

At 4 a.m. the explosion took place as arranged, as we knew it must, for the Japanese, gallant little souls! broke their engagements to none, and showed their backs to nothing. We immediately stood to arms, and in five minutes' time were running through the burning gateway to fulfil our share in the general plan. The Japanese were seen to be engaged in some half hearted street fighting, which was becoming rapidly less; and organised resistance soon ceased. Next in, were our marines, and the Chinese regiment; after them the French. The manner in which these excitable men behaved was almost contemptible. They planted their little tricolours all along the south wall, they shook each other by the hand, six buglers mounted the wall and blew a fanfare of trumpets, and finally, to their shame be it said, they fired volleys into masses of fugitives pouring out of the west gate, among whom were many women.

By their behaviour, an outsider would have judged that to them, and to them alone, belonged the credit of the city's fall. For some hours the various troops were engaged in clearing the city, and the villages on the north side of it, which were full of snipers who kept up a brisk fire until turned out of it by the Japs, who pushed right on and helped the Russians take the city fort, which was the last point of resistance. The Russians and Germans on the other side of the river, had experienced the same serious opposition on the 13th, and had but partially succeeded, like ourselves; but in a similar manner the morning of the 14th brought better luck, and by noon on that day the city with all its surroundings was undisputedly in the hands of the Allies.

To the Japanese belongs the lion's share of the credit, the Russians and British probably being their most able assistants. This victory, the most costly as it was the most decisive, was also the turning-point from defence to attack,—in fact, it must always remain the most important movement in the whole campaign, opening the way, as it did, for the advance on Pekin, which for several reasons could never have been begun until the Chinese had been forced to evacuate their great stronghold. The severity of the fighting may best be judged from the casualty list, which numbered 775, of whom the greater number were Japanese and Russians, the remainder; being mainly composed of Americans, British, and French.

The Naval Brigade's share in the day's fighting was alluded to in the general's despatches in a most complimentary manner, and the services rendered by the company who went to the assistance of the 9th U.S. infantry, were also gracefully acknowledged by the American Senate.

CHAPTER 9

Scenes in the Captured City

When once resistance had ceased there was time to look about one, and it was a scene worth remembering that met the eyes, if only it had been possible to shut out some of the hideous effects of the last two days' fighting. From the top of the wall one saw a large, densely-built city which at first only seemed to boast of three roads, one encircling the whole, and the other two equally dividing it into four parts, meeting at the centre, where their intersection was marked by an imposing-looking structure, which might have been either *pagoda* or gate. In its most peaceful days it is improbable that anyone thought it beautiful. "Striking" is perhaps the word which would have been employed by a globe-trotter.

However, Tientsin was unlike itself on the morning of July 14, and had it ever been striking, it was then doubly so. The first thing to be noticed was the gate of entry, which was blazing furiously, together with what remained of a fine *pagoda* which had been built on the top of it. The latter had been literally pulverised by shells, and had been burning for some hours. Though nearly burnt out, it caused great inconvenience to the troops, who were compelled for the time to lie in its vicinity. A glance at the wall also bore testimony to the accuracy of the Allies' artillery fire; and although the projectiles were for the most part too small to inflict any great structural damage, yet here and there the ramparts had been swept dear away for several feet at a time. Twenty-three shell marks were distinctly visible on the south gate walls, and on what remained of its *pagoda*, and it must be admitted that the Chinese who defended this and the neighbouring portions of the wall, showed a tenacity not to be gainsaid.

It is doubtful whether, with the exception of a few in the suburbs and prison, the enemy lost as many as thirty men from rifle fire on

MAIN ROAD—TIENTSIN

the whole of the 13th; for the wall was so thick, and the loopholes so small, that even the possibility of a stray bullet finding a fleshy resting-place was almost precluded.

Shells, however, had done their work elsewhere, as destructively to material and perhaps more so to life, as they had done on the walls. They had burst promiscuously when once they had passed over the walls; and from what the Allies had seen of promiscuous shelling it was not held to be particularly dangerous; but here the conditions were somewhat different. Hardly a shell could pitch without landing on a roof, and then the houses were of a much more inflammable nature and densely packed with human beings.

From this, and from the general appearance of the town, it may be assumed that the actual damage done in the last twenty-four hours' incessant shelling was nearly equal to that which was the effect of many days' dilatory bombardment on the part of the Chinese. The casualties, which were the result of it, were undoubtedly heavier than those which occurred in the settlements, from a similar cause, during the whole month's siege. The further one went into the city, the more horrible were the scenes with which one was confronted. Shrapnel, common shell, and lyddite had spared no one; every type was to be found there lying where they fell, killed, one might almost say, by an accident,—male and female, old men and little naked children. Brutalised as one gets when fighting against a merciless foe, it makes one shudder even now to look back on it!

The numbers were largest towards the north gate, but in this case men were looking on the bodies of their proper enemies, the paid soldiers of the hostile government; and, after gazing on the scene just portrayed (one hundred times more lightly than the reality, out of respect for the feelings of those who peruse this chapter) there was for them no room for sentiment. Rather sad too was the sight of the ten or twelve corpses, all laid on hastily improvised stretchers, to be seen in most of the courtyards of the Yamens, which had evidently been turned into hospitals for the occasion. Some of these had been attended to while still alive, but the bandages were put on in a careless and slovenly manner, and testified neither to the skill nor the attention of the native doctors. No wounded were found in these places, which points to the fact that the Chinese, even in their hasty retreat, retained some of the cohesion without which any body of armed men quickly becomes a rabble.

There was plenty of evidence to prove that anarchy had reigned supreme for the last day or two; many houses had been forcibly entered, and their less valuable contents strewn about the streets; and the severed heads of several Boxers were to be seen hanging to poles by their pigtails, which showed dissension had been rife between the Regulars and their fanatical Auxiliaries. All sanitary arrangements had been disregarded, and a most unpleasant reek of decomposing garbage offended the senses at every turn.

The fire brigade, if such a thing existed, had naturally decamped on the fall of the south gate, and the Allies found the town on fire in a dozen places, notably in the N.-W. and S.-E. quarters. The reason that these two quarters suffered most heavily in this respect, while the N.-E. and S.-W. quarters enjoyed comparative immunity, is easily explained, when it is understood that the majority of the Allies' guns were facing the N.-W. to S.-E. diagonal, so that should a shell just top the wall, it perhaps created a fire in the S.-E. corner, whereas, if elevated for another three or four hundred yards, it had a similar chance of doing so in the N.-E. corner.

There was a good deal to be done, one of the most important things being the barring of ingress to anyone but Europeans. To ensure this, all the gates were guarded, and all outgoing Chinamen were searched, and permitted to go, while all candidates for admission were searched and turned back.

A rather grim incident occurred during the police work at the north gate. The Japanese were guarding the bridge outside the walls when two Chinamen came along, dressed like *coolies*, and begged for admission. This was at once refused; whereupon the two men tried to shove past the guard. Of course such temerity was fatal; they were leapt upon and thrown to the earth, after which they were searched; on each were found arms and ammunition, and both were immediately "despatched," and their bodies hurled into the river. Someone near by, expressed the opinion that it was rather an arbitrary method of dealing with them; but by every rule of war their fate was deserved. They were spies with arms concealed on them, and by their eagerness to get inside the gates, it may be supposed that some plan was to be carried through to the detriment of the troops in possession, which was only frustrated by their timely end. It was, however, noticeable that later candidates carried themselves with more submission than the two whose fate had been just witnessed.

The first thing that the British did, when the city had been cleared, was to seize a number of the *junks* which crowded the river along the northern wall, as well as two steamers, one a convenient little launch, the other a paddle steamer which, though tried for some time, eventually proved useless. The *junks* were expected to be of great assistance in the forthcoming advance on Pekin, and although some were too big for the higher reaches of the river, yet many proved of inestimable value in conjunction with the transport arrangements for the above named expedition. Guards were placed on every gate, and by two o'clock it was possible to withdraw some of the troops to the settlement.

No sooner was personal safety assured than the city became full of people, all bent on plunder,—in fact the looting of Tientsin had begun. Loot, a word which had seemed to have died a natural death in favour of "commandeer," is only a polite way of talking about the act of transferring some one else's property to one's own pocket, or as it happened in this case, to one's own *rickshaw*. It was now the one topic of conversation, the one aim of every one able to roam the streets of Tientsin, unfettered by orders or scruples; and it is safe to say that every one, except the British soldiers and sailors, and other troops on duty, indulged in this pursuit at the earliest opportunity and to the fullest extent. This is not meant to mislead people into thinking that the British did no looting, but merely to point out that at first it was the intention of the British authorities not to allow it, a moral desire which was at last overcome by the example set by every one else, including civilians, who had taken no share in the fighting, but who saw a chance to recompense themselves for any loss they had sustained by Chinese shells.

When the British forces did start, however, nearly everything of any value had been taken; and as only two days were allowed, there was no time to search under floors, and in hollow walls, which were the hiding places for the bulk of the hidden bullion. Be this as it may, it can safely be said that there were but few in the brigade who had not the word "loot" lightly engraved on their hearts by the 15th, by which time it was proposed to divide the city into spheres of influence under military command. The word "lightly" is used advisedly, for their looting was of the gentlemanly order, and not accompanied by threats, outrage, and even murder, which was unfortunately the case with at least two of the other European contingents. It was extraordinary to see the trust reposed in the Japanese, British, and Americans. The householders would ask for flags, and a guard to protect them from some of the others; and hundreds of little home-made flags fluttered from the doorways and windows in every direction.

One writer on the subject remarks with surprise, on the number of Japanese and French flags that were shown. A little thought would have shown him that they are in the first place ridiculously easy to imitate, the first one needing but a red blob on a white ground, and the second a little red ink, a clear white stripe, and a stripe of the ordinary blue ink, make a very fair tricolour. The first were also shown with the earnest desire to propitiate, the second because, not being able to make British or American ensigns, they thought that any protector was perhaps better than none. Now so much has been said and written on the great evils of looting, and especially on the looting of Tientsin, that a summing up of the case by one who was to a certain extent "in the know" can hardly be inappropriate or uninteresting.

To begin with, the evidence of many of those who have written articles to the papers in denunciation of the authorities, or of the allied troops, is worth but little, as it is more than probable that, by infringing some of the rules, they lost what they themselves had looted, and their bitter feelings may be accounted for by the fact that although it is occasionally "*better to have loved and lost than never to have loved at all,*" it is certainly not better to have looted and forfeited, than never to have looted at all. Thus a proportion must be deducted from the ranks of "conscientious objectors" whose argument is that the transferment of someone else's property to oneself is never permissible, except it take the form of an exchange, a sale, or a gift; also that the recognised law in civilised warfare is that looters will be shot.

On the other side of the argument are to be found of course all the participators, and a multitude of people who envy the latter their good fortune, but whose envy does not go far enough to cause them to act protector of the down-trodden, through the medium of the press. These very rightly say, that in the first place the Tientsin looting was not an incident in civilised warfare at all; "devilishly cruel" has been already applied to the Chinese in this book, but the superlative has not yet been coined which would adequately describe the treatment of women and the wounded who fell into their hands. Then again the power to "save face" is so highly thought of in China, that had Tientsin not been looted, and had it not been decided to alter the face of the city in other ways as well, it is probable that one of the most valuable lessons of the whole war would have remained untaught.

Another excellent excuse was the fact that quite a third of the city was in flames, in which case, had no looting taken place, thousands of valuables would now be no more, whereas they have gone to gladden the hearts of the womenfolk, and to brighten the rooms of every nation of any importance from Japan westward to America. After all, there is precedent without end, for in nearly every instance where a city has fallen by direct assault, and where there has been only flight, not surrender, on the part of the defenders, the town has been sacked. The force of example need hardly be quoted as an excuse, because it amounts to an admittance of moral weakness, and in no case do two wrongs make a right.

But war itself is hardly an ideal state of affairs, and it is harsh to blame a little easing up of discipline within strict limits, after a bloody and bitter conflict, brought to a successful issue solely by the discipline and devotion of the troops engaged. If further argument is necessary, it remains to be said that by far the greatest thieves were the Chinese themselves, who as soon as they found they were not noticed in the general scramble, were untiring in their endeavours to make their fortune at the expense of others; and these men, not even excepting the civilians from the settlement, were undoubtedly those whose measure of success was greatest. As a proof of how partial the sack of the city really was, a well-known Chinese Tientsin banker remarked quite recently, that of thirty-eight banks of importance, and the treasury, only the latter and one of the former had been touched, thanks to the innate "wile" of the owners, who invariably take the greatest pains to put their wealth out of sight.

Given the desire and power to loot, it only remains to be told the method employed by the various nations, and for the loot to be described, to gather a fairly accurate idea of the scene. The arrangement at first had been to allow looting to be proceeded with until noon on the 15th, when it would be suppressed; and all loot found in the possession of people who had broken the rule would be forfeited to a common fund to go to the troops who had done the fighting.

To begin with the British: there were bluejackets, marines, infantry-men, engineers, Indians, and the Chinese regiment, most of whom were working in parties, which in many cases had officers with them. In this they differed from any other nation, and it was a wise step to take. It at least ensured the absence of the slightest brutality, and it minimised the risk of collision with other troops, which was always to be reckoned with in the then state of men's minds. A dispute at that time over a pawnshop, a fur cloak, or an ornament, must have had very serious consequences, as the men were all fully armed, and each nationality was as suspicious and jealous as possible of the others. As a matter of fact the British troops proved comparatively unsuccessful as looters. They started late, behaved so quietly, and seemed to have no idea of the value of anything, except actual money or *sycee*, which latter it may be explained was bar silver moulded into 41b. ingots worth about £7. 10s. each. Then again, although either the treasury or the salt commissioners' Yamen might have fallen into their hands, they allowed themselves to be passed by the Japanese and Americans respectively.

The British civilians, however, supplied all deficiencies and made most successful hauls. In order not to hurt innocent and "conscientious objectors'" feelings, it must be mentioned that only those who looted are spoken of, and not all and sundry, as might have been assumed from the foregoing sentence. They, of course, knew the very houses to go to, they knew the value of every article, they had their own servants, and in some cases their own conveyances to carry their gear from the spot where it was found to their residences, in fact for them not to have made the best of it would have shown a lack of grasp of the situation to be wondered at.

The Japanese were stern but humane looters; they saw what they wanted, took it and went, and unless molested or baulked they hurt no one. The Americans were also a free-and-easy lot of fellows; they too demanded, not asked, and they too were harmless if not crossed. It may be said that the same humane line of action that was followed by these three nations during the whole campaign was carried out to the letter in the demoralising times during the looting of Tientsin. It is not proposed to discuss the ways of the other nations; not that it is to be supposed for one instant that they are all tarred with one brush.

For instance, the Russians and Germans did not participate in the looting of Tientsin proper, and the Austrians and Italians were so small in numbers, that their looting power suffered in comparison to the troops of other countries; while to enlarge on the undoubted prowess possessed by *l'infanterie de la marine,* although it would only be to endorse what has already been said, would probably raise a storm of indignation and gesticulation to which the author has neither time nor inclination to reply. The supply of loot itself was nearly if not quite equal to the demand. *Sycee* abounded, furs and silks were so common that anything except sable and mink were trodden underfoot, and none but the most beautiful embroideries were thought worth the space they occupied. Rolls of the most beautiful silk, worth pounds, were treated as if they had been calico; astrakhan, squirrel, and fox skins were left to the Chinese who had been too tired to run away.

Silver watches simply bored one, and on asking the time from a stranger he would probably give you a couple of this type of time-piece. Gold and enamel watches were there also; watches set with pearls, and eighty guinea gold repeaters, were all to be got; but these mostly came out of houses, not from the shops. Of silver articles of jewellery there were literally sacksful, but only the lucky few managed to get hold of gold rings with jewels in them, of which there was a more limited supply. In real Jade bracelets and ornaments there were several fortunes, but the ignorance of the men for the most part was responsible for these being either thrown down, or left to fall into the hands of some lucky officer.

Even the looting had to end, and by noon on June 15th there were pickets out guarding the approaches to the British concession, with orders to allow no one to retain any plunder except French subjects, whose consul or commander had not fallen in with the general plan. Many curious things happened, some folk coming in with dignity, striving for a place; on their features could be seen "Avarice satisfied" as plainly as possible. Others, in ignorance of the law, came and conversed with the officer of the picket, and assured him that there was plenty left, and if only they had a hay-cart instead of a broken rick-shaw, the former would have been just as full as the latter.

On being apprised of the state of affairs, entreaty and invective held the ring in turn against all corners for quite a time. Some, more wily, who possessed a knowledge of French, tried to palm themselves off as Frenchmen. About this is a curious story to be told, first mentioning that a similar story is current, which had quite a different ending, but which, in all other respects, tallies with this one. Several *rickshaws* came along under the charge of two or three men, who, when stopped by a military picket, jabbered away in French, shrugged their shoulders, lifted their hands, and twirled their *moustachios* to such an extent that they were allowed to pass; but, unfortunately, they "struck" a naval picket, under the command of a very small, but very officious midshipman, who considered it to be nothing less than sinful to allow such a haul to escape his clutches, so he ordered the party to barracks for investigation.

They didn't want to go a bit, and at last their French broke down when they had got halfway, and found that, owing to the young officer having but an imperfect knowledge of the language, it was impossible—quite impossible—to persuade him to alter his mind by arguing in French. Finally, the loot and its erstwhile owners parted company, the latter swearing volubly, but in English. And yet there are people who say that the British Naval officer's greatest failing is his want of knowledge in foreign tongues! Incidents of the same sort followed each other in quick succession, and by the night of the 15th the looting of Tientsin was at an end.

CHAPTER 10

Preparations for Final Advance

Much had now been done towards ensuring the safety of European life and property in the North, but much yet remained to do. To begin with, the fate of the Legations in Pekin was still unknown, and all the last runners to get through were the bearers of more and more hopeless messages, which contained prayers for a speedy relief; and as the safety, or rather want of safety, of the ministers had been responsible for every move on the part of the Allies, it will be seen that, even apart from political considerations, and they were many, the relief of Pekin was now a matter of the greatest importance; in fact, it was merely the end to which all other operations had been the means. The Taku Forts had been taken, not because a rising at Tientsin was feared, but because it was necessary to have a base resting on the sea, from which supplies and men could be sent to Admiral Seymour, who, of course, had the safety of the ministers almost solely at heart, when he at first commenced his splendid but unavailing attempt to reach the capital.

After that first success, we have seen how Tientsin settlements were attacked by the enemy, and how, after a gallant defence, they were relieved by the column from the forts, who had been reinforced from Port Arthur and Hong-Kong. Immediately after—in fact, at the same time as all this was taking place—we have followed Seymour's march and ultimate retirement, and the relief of Tientsin brings us to his relief, which followed on the next day. Then comes the second siege of Tientsin, with its extraordinary aggressive defence, during which all outlying Chinese arsenals and positions were stormed and taken, until at last Tientsin city alone remained.

This stronghold itself was attacked and fell, and there seemed likely to be a prolonged rest on both sides, for it had already been proved that to advance on Pekin with anything but an overwhelming force was useless, and it may be confidently asserted that the Chinese would not have resumed offensive tactics for some time, on account of extreme exhaustion—the word being used in the sense in which it is applicable to an army, rather than in its physical meaning. But all the operations had taken time, and during the month that had elapsed from the commencement of the war, troops were hurrying from Kiel, Marseilles, Spezzia, Fiume, India, the Philippines, Japan, and Port Arthur, and a number of these had already landed at Taku.

It became evident that the sailors' work as infantrymen had finished, and they once more found themselves employed as "Handymen," mounting two 4-in. Q.F. on field carriages, getting junks ready for the army, unloading lighters, doing all the fatigue work—in fact, tidying up, so that the soldiers might have a flying start. This kind of thing represents the dregs of active service, but the men had the satisfaction of knowing that they were going to be represented by six guns and a battalion of marines, and they worked to such purpose that it may be doubted whether any army corps has ever landed to find such a perfect preparation, or their initial task in such a nearly finished condition.

As many men as could be spared went down to their ships to recruit their health for the fortnight before the advance was to commence, but a company were shortly recalled to Tientsin, and received orders to construct a battery on the south face of the settlements, to ward off a possible attack from the south-westward, where it was reported the enemy were massing in great numbers. Work was commenced on the night of arrival, and by the next evening, by dint of much labour, the following guns were in position, ready for use: seven 6-pr. Q.F., three 9-pr. M.L. field-guns, three Maxims, and a five-barrelled Nordenfelt. It might be termed a scratch pack, but such was their position, that they were capable of holding off any number of infantry, and might have successfully dealt with artillery up to three thousand yards.

The first British troops to arrive were the 7th Rajputs, and some of the 1st Bengal Lancers; they caused a great impression by their soldierly bearing, and were eyed with curiosity by the other European soldiers. After them came Sikhs, Bengal cavalry, Madras pioneers, and Baluchis, all of whom impressed the onlooker as preferable allies rather than antagonists. The troops of other nations were quickly on the scene, and Tientsin gradually became a huge camp of armed men. The life was not an unenjoyable one; fresh food in plenty was again obtainable, the native hawkers came back in small numbers with fruit and vegetables, and in the evenings two bands played for about an hour.

There was also a prospect of some perfectly quiet nights, which had been the great exception for some time past, and which remained in the prospective stage even now, for the mosquitoes worried one more than the sound of a rifle or shell fire; and while one can get used to the latter evil in but a short time, it is next to impossible to accustom oneself to the attacks of myriads of the former, whose bites are irritable for days. An interesting piece of work was the discovery and reclaiming of Seymour's 9-pr. M.L. guns, which had been thrown into the river during the retirement. They were found in an arsenal inside the city when it fell, and were dragged back in triumph to the settlement, where they were painted Khaki colour and placed on the steps of the Town Hall, which they still adorn, (1905).

It is not to be supposed that the troops had an easy time; they were constantly drilling, the horses were being got into condition after their voyages, portable filters were made from *congues* and sand and charcoal, the former being obtained and prepared—in fact, everything possible was done to ensure a start at the first moment that the Allies' numbers would reach the required total, said by some to be 25,000, by others 40,000 at least. The British went a long way ahead in the matter of *junks*, for they secured a *junk* yard with about eighty new *junks* in it—an extraordinary capture, considering the way in which other nations usually forestalled us in matters of this sort. As a matter of fact, only about half the *junks* were available for use, owing to the fact that they, being new, opened their seams and sank immediately they were floated; however, the ones which had been taken on the river provided ample accommodation for the British contingent.

The work of collecting *junks* off the river was a task not looked forward to by either officers or men, consisting, as it did, of turning whole families out into the banks, from what had been their sole living place; but the orders were to get *junks*, and empty ones are not found floating about in wartime even in China. One certainly was seen floating by itself, and, being of a suitable nature and size, it was immediately boarded. It was, however, tenanted by eight corpses of people who had met violent deaths,—and was therefore allowed to go on floating. Sights like this, and others yet more horrible, were only too common, and it is not to be wondered at that the "*junk* parties," as they were called, were glad when their labours finished, and a sufficient number had been collected.

The allied commanders usually met every day to discuss their plans, and to fix the probable date of starting, when an event happened which altered all existing arrangements. A message arrived, which again urged the necessity of the utmost despatch, or it would be too late. This, at least, showed that things were fearfully critical inside the capital, and it found a responsive echo in the commanders' breasts, so that it was decided to leave Tientsin on August 5th, which date was afterwards altered to the 4th.

Of course the advance had been preceded by a reconnaissance to ascertain where the enemy intended making his first stand, to discover his numbers, and to make him, if possible, disclose the strength of his position. This had all been done by the Japanese on the 21st of July, and when at last the little army moved out of the settlement, it was felt that everything possible had been done to ensure the success of the enterprise.

When the relief force had left, the troops in the settlement, consisting of Japanese, Indians, and a few Americans, French, and Russians, and a small naval detachment, still had plenty to do; scares began again immediately, and a new system of defence had to be arranged. The British were busily employed in perfecting the south battery, and all the other nations were working at similar tasks.

The lines had been greatly enlarged since the fall of the city, and included all the space enclosed by the mud wall, which encircled the native city as well as the settlements, and which was held by Japanese at several points on the right bank of the river—notably at the Taku gate and the Hi-Kwan-Su arsenal. The suburbs on the other bank were held by the Russians, who also occupied the flanking forts to the northwestward, as far as, and including, the Hsi-Ku arsenal.

Down at Taku the utmost activity prevailed The 6th U.S. cavalry disembarked and proceeded to Tientsin, but were not able to join in the advance, owing to the condition of their horses; the Italian Bersaglieri also landed, and shortly arrived in Tientsin. They looked workmanlike and smart, and their rate of marching was really astonishing.

Another thing which occupied a good deal of attention at Taku was the completing of two 4-in. Q.F. guns on improved carriages of Captain Percy Scott's original design. These eventually turned up too late, and although they were sent to the front, they were never brought into action.

News was received from the front by field telegraph, but a more certain way was getting it first-hand from the midshipman in charge of the *Barfleur's* steam pinnace, who had orders to keep touch with the army, to bring back sick and wounded, and to keep the river clear for the peaceable passage of *junks*. This involved plenty of hard work, during which one young officer got a bad touch of sunstroke and was sent to hospital; but another took his place, and the excitement and responsibility served to make hard work seem very pleasant.

For the benefit of those readers who, not understanding what a "manned and armed" boat is, and who might reasonably be inclined to think that an unarmed boat would be useless and even dangerous, it must be explained that the boat carried a 3-pr. Q.F. gun in the bows and a Maxim in the stern, which would have enabled her to hold off any inconsiderable parties of the enemy who might be met with.

As bad luck would have it, the boat drew too much water for the upper reaches of the river, so that it was impossible to go much above Yangtsun; she was also very slow, and when no longer able to communicate with the army, the need of her services soon ceased.

One incident occurred at this time which showed the true feeling of some of the Foreign troops towards the British. Just above the English settlement was a pontoon bridge, guarded and worked by a French picket, who were always extremely obstinate about opening it after dark. One night the steam pinnace came down from Yangtsun about one o'clock, with, as usual, several sick and wounded on board; and on hailing the picket and asking that the bridge might be opened, the officer met with a flat refusal. He replied that it was a case of necessity, as there were men who might die for want of assistance on board; but a corporal replied: "Oh yes, you've always got wounded, haven't you?"

Rather angry, the English officer replied that he would report him to his superior officer in the morning, whereupon he was told that he better go and do it himself, and that he might stay on the other side of the bridge all night unless he opened it himself. This he attempted to do, but the heavy planks, which had to be drawn from side to side, proved to be too much for him and the two men, which were all that could be allowed out of the boat. At last he demanded that if assistance was not forthcoming in two minutes' time he would destroy the bridge by throwing the planks into the river, which would have to be replaced in the morning. Beyond oaths and gesticulations, no reply was vouchsafed from the other bank, so, at the expiration of two minutes, over went number one plank after a great struggle.

Terrific gesticulations and fearful oaths, followed by another refusal to the demand for assistance, led to the disappearance of plank number two, leaving only number three. This appeared to sober the corporal somewhat, and he, with four men, crossed the remaining plank and dragged it over, leaving just room for the boat. Of course the officer and bluejackets embarked, and told the Frenchmen to get to their side of the river over the boat; but this led to such a storm of abuse from them, who had evidently imagined that the British in their turn were going to replace the plank, that the watch was again requisitioned, and, at the expiration of the same interval of time, the boat went ahead, leaving two of the five in safety, two in the water, and one cursing on the wrong side of the river. Representations were made to the proper authorities next day, and not only was a new bridge, capable of more easy manipulation, built, but on subsequent passages the officer of the boat met with nothing but civility.

A similar unpleasantness occurred to the first midshipman of the boat—only on this occasion it was with the Russians, and diplomacy, instead of high-handed dealing, in this case gained the day. The same argument about right-of-way began one day, and it was not until several hours had been wasted that the boat was allowed to pass. Determined that this sort of thing should not happen again, the midshipman, on his next arrival at Tientsin, obtained an imposing-looking blue envelope, and having filled it with bulky papers, wrote the Russian general's name on it.

Once more there was the same difficulty, but after a lot of trouble the soldiers on guard brought an officer who talked just enough English to understand what the envelope purported to be. He was immediately all politeness, and begged that he might have the supposed despatches, which he would forward immediately; but, as they were not despatches at all—and even if they had been, the officer might have forgotten to open the bridge after all—the midshipman, while thanking him for his kindness, begged him not to press the point, as he had had the strictest orders not to let them out of sight until safely delivered. The bridge swung open, the boat passed through, and so most probably did the "despatches," which were flung into the river when out of sight.

Three or four days after the army's departure, the most extravagant stories went round that 40,000 Boxers with guns were coming to attack the settlement in a day or two. But few people believed this effort of some one's diseased imagination. It must be owned, however, that another exodus of natives took place, many of whom were notably faithful to their European masters, and who had in the past risked much for their sake. At any rate, so persistent did the rumours become, that it was decided to send a reconnaissance out to the south-westward to gain some idea of their truth. Accordingly, a force of cavalry—chiefly Americans, but partly Indian—was sent out to discover what truth there might be in the matter.

They rode for seven miles without seeing any enemy, but, on approaching some villages at this distance, a heavy fire was opened on them from Rifles and *Jingals*, and it became certain that the villages were held in force.

It was noticed, however, that there were no Imperial troops among the enemy, who showed no signs of organisation, though even a horde of well-armed peasants would be able to make things very unpleasant for cavalry in a village; and having discovered what was wanted, the force retired to Tientsin. During the retirement one of the American horses took fright, and threw its rider heavily, who lay stunned within short range of the enemy, and, had it not been for the presence of mind of Lieutenant Gaussen of the 1st Bengal Lancers, who rode back, picked him up, and carried him to safety, a regrettable incident might have occurred. On the night of the reconnaissance several shots were fired into the Hsi-Ku arsenal by snipers, and a Japanese sentry was killed: shots were fired at other points also, and it was clear that the enemy were going to pursue their old sniping tactics if left in the vicinity.

Therefore, acting on the news which had been gathered, a little expedition was determined on, the results of which might be expected to clear the neighbourhood altogether of any enemy. The strength of the force was about 1,500, consisting of 700 Indian infantry, 200 Japanese infantry, 500 of the 6th U.S. cavalry, 100 Bengal lancers, and two guns. The movement was meant to be a secret, but details leaked out, and, as the Naval Brigade were so small, they found, to their disgust, that they had been left out. However, they were represented by two officers, who simply appeared to "happen" upon the troops as they started, and who attached themselves as non-official gallopers to the staff. The men of the brigade were told that they were much too valuable to be thrown away as infantrymen, but the sailors refused to see things in that light, arguing that, having borne the brunt of the campaign, and having suffered some four hundred casualties, they ought to be allowed to see the thing through.

The plan of action was that the guns and infantry should turn the Boxers out of each village in turn, and that every time an opportunity occurred, the cavalry should charge them as they fled. The first part of the programme was carried out perfectly, but the second part failed in some degree through an extraordinary mistake on the part of the American cavalry, who, on being ordered to charge, dismounted and poured in a singularly ineffective fire from their carbines, probably accounting for twenty men where they might have accounted for two hundred. The Bengal lancers, few as they were, rectified the error to some extent by executing a brilliant charge, in which one hundred and eighty of the enemy were slain. The ground was almost perfect for cavalry work—a long flat sandy plain, intersected here and there by ditches, but so shallow that the majority would be little more than a foot in depth—and the only excuse the Americans could urge would be that either the order was misunderstood by them, or that their training has been on the lines of mounted infantry.

The day ended in the utter rout of the Chinese, and in the destruction of seven villages, which further forwarded the work of decentralisation. The Allies' total loss was under fifty; that of the enemy possibly four hundred. Several prisoners were also taken and brought back to the settlement, where they were tried by a mixed tribunal on two or three charges. Some were executed, others released, while the remainder became servants in the different barracks, and performed any odd jobs which required attending to. This absolutely ended any fighting around Tientsin, and the work of the troops in garrison gradually got lighter and lighter, until affairs reached the verge of boredom. The heads of departments had plenty to do. For instance, four nations started field-force post-offices, which, by-the-bye, were largely patronised by stamp-collectors; and the governing of Tientsin city also took much careful consideration and management.

It was wonderful to notice the difference in the place since it had fallen. The streets were positively clean in places—no dead bodies, no obnoxious smells, any number of inhabitants, not even any looting. All this made the place almost unrecognisable. The extreme easiness of duty, and the fact that time began to hang heavily on the hands of officers and men, were responsible for the more energetic spirits beginning to look around them for some pastime which would afford both amusement and exercise.

In the course of conversation with civilians it became known that the autumn Snipe were now in, and that good bags of Longbills might be made in the vicinity with a little trouble. The primary trouble of finding the birds was obviated by one of the officers of an Indian lament, who had noticed a likely marsh while out on the aforementioned reconnaissance. This proved to be only about a mile and a half outside the lines, and as the whole district was now absolutely quiet, several officers took advantage of the opportunity to not only keep themselves fit, but to replenish the larder with good fat Snipe, which were a most acceptable change for breakfast after a somewhat protracted course of the everlasting sardine.

Every afternoon several guns visited the marsh which had been the scene of one of the earlier combats, and in addition to bringing back sometimes ten or twelve couple of birds, such articles as rifles, *jingals*, and sword bayonets were frequently added to the bag. How enjoyable it was to be killing, or even frightening, something a little less imposing when in the bag than human beings; and how absurd it seemed to be once more using a 12-bore instead of a rifle or 12-pounder on the actual ground which only a month ago was strewn with the bodies of men who had fallen in action! Needless to say long practice with the one weapon had not improved one's shooting powers with the other, but it is interesting to record that the last shot fired at Tientsin was a peaceable one excepting only those occasions on which the Allied troops, tiring of fighting no one, turned their weapons on each other. At last, just as August ended, the first part of the Naval Brigade returned from the front, which proved to be the beginning of the end for the senior service.

CHAPTER 11

Advance to Pekin

The force which left the settlement on the afternoon of August 4th, was by many considered to be far too small for the task in front of it; it only numbered between 16,000 and 17,000 men, and suffered from many disadvantages common to mixed forces. There were so many chiefs, with as many different ideas; there was a great lack of efficient transport among some of the forces; the weather was either scorching hot or very wet; and, finally, there were supposed to be four times as many Chinese between Tientsin and Pekin as European troops which had left the former place; but when everything had been said and done, there was the same desire burning in each breast of the 16,000, and there was a keen rivalry between the forces, which plainly told that each would exert himself to the utmost for the honour of his country.

The start was hardly auspicious, for although the weather was perfect when the last column left Tientsin, before the first companies had reached Hsi-Ku arsenal, where was to be the first night's bivouac, the rain was coming down in torrents; and as the men were without tents, the prospect was altogether miserable. With the certainty of a general engagement on the morrow, the troops did the best for themselves that they could, and lay down in the mud near the posts which they were to occupy in the morning's fighting. The Chinese position lay to the direct front, at a distance of under four miles; it was immensely strong, and had been chosen with such care that every eventuality seemed to have been allowed for.

Unfortunately, as had already happened so often, the utter want of good officers, and the limited amount of backbone remaining in his troops, rendered all the skilful dispositions of the Chinese general of no avail, and all his miles of entrenchments, the work of weeks, useless. The Japanese lay on the right of the allied force, the British in the centre, and the Russians on the left,—the Americans, who were to have worked in the centre, did not turn up in time to take any serious part in the engagement.

At half-past four, the ball was opened by the Chinese artillery, who began to fire aimlessly in the direction of Hsi-Ku arsenal. Shortly after this, the Japanese pushed straight to the front, and in face of some slight opposition, stormed the outlying Chinese trenches; the enemy withdrew to their main defences, and the battle opened with severe musketry fire from both sides. The Japanese artillery was hard at work from the very beginning, but the British guns had as yet taken no part. At last the Royal Artillery came into action near the river embankment, and as usual they did not forget their wonderful parade-ground movements under fire; it might have been a competition, so smartly was every action performed. They immediately came under a hot fire, and lost a few men; and although their shooting was everything that could be desired, the position was not a favourable one, and they soon moved away to the left.

The enemy's guns presently began to show signs of being over-matched, and an infantry advance became possible. This the Japanese led, and with extraordinary gallantry swept right down on to the trenches, which were simply blazing with hostile fire, taking the first one with the bayonet, and then waiting for reinforcements and a short rest. The advance became general, and the Chinese guns began to shift their positions preparatory to withdrawing, and, at length beginning to realise that they were beaten, the infantry became more and more unsteady, and also evinced a strong desire to be off. Two more brilliantly executed attacks transformed their ideas into action, and they commenced to flee.

The cavalry was immediately launched at the fugitives, and the Japanese getting among the retreating artillery, succeeded in capturing six guns. The Indian cavalry fared hardly so well. A change seemed to have come over the Chinese officers, and for once they retreated with, instead of before, their men, and managed to keep some sort of formation and discipline among their companies. Three times the cavalry were forced to sheer off from the compact bodies of riflemen, who seemed to instinctively understand that foot soldiers in close order have nothing to fear from horsemen, and time after time they turned to their front, and received the lancers with such steadiness that it would have been foolhardiness to press the charge right home.

An opportunity, however, at length came, and it was fully demonstrated that broken infantry stand no chance whatever against some of the finest horse soldiers in the world, who, no matter how long they have been compelled to delay their attack, had proved themselves capable of waiting for the supreme moment when cohesion is lost in the ranks of the defeated, and a defeat becomes a rout. Even when the day was irretrievably lost, here and there parties of the enemy offered a stubborn resistance, doubtless with a view to the escape of their remaining guns. The naval guns had taken but a small part in this important action; but although labouring under several disadvantages, the work they did was rather surprising. For many reasons, notably that they had to keep near the river in order to be ready for instant embarkation, also that their chief role was meant to be that of a siege battery, the guns were left at a prohibitive range for the ordinary field guns.

In addition to this the enemy were not visible to the men laying their guns; but by firing on a bearing, the range being taken by officers up ladders and trees, they managed to create considerable havoc among the groups of the flying enemy at the beginning of the retreat. The Chinese fled towards Pekin, leaving a strong body of infantry, to check pursuit, in the village of Peitsang itself. These gave a lot of trouble, but were eventually ousted by the Japanese, who indeed may almost lay claim to the whole credit of the victory,—the hardest-fought battle, and the one with the most important results, of any that took place with the China field force, as the relieving army was called. An attempt was made to pursue the enemy, but eight hours' fighting had taken the sting out of the horses; and when it was absolutely certain that there was no chance of any counter attack, it was decided to bivouac for the night.

The Allies lost in this engagement nearly 500 men, more than half of whom were Japanese. The Chinese lost about the same number, in addition to eight guns, their camp, and large quantities of food and ammunition. During the night the troops lay down near the site of the Chinese camp, the French and Russians joining forces with the remainder, as the ground on their side of the river was too difficult to negotiate in any extended formation. A squadron of Bengal lancers was sent out during the night to bring news of the enemy, and on their return they reported that they were in force at Yangtsun, some 12 miles further on. Acting on this, the whole force moved at six o'clock, leaving 50 men of the 7th Rajputs under an English subaltern and a native major, to form a guard on the line of communications.

A march of 10 miles brought the Allies again within touch of the enemy, who were in great force, and once more in a well-chosen, formidable position. Their point covered nearly two miles, and their infantry were protected by two lines of carefully dug trenches, which for the most part lay along the railway embankment, and the face of the village on the opposite bank to the fortified city of Yangtsun. This time the British and Americans were given the post of honour, with the Russians in close support, the Japanese resting after their magnificent impetuosity of the day before. The way for the attack was prepared by the artillery, of which the Allies had three batteries in action, British six guns, Americans a like number, and the Russians four. It was their duty to crush eighteen hostile guns, and then to turn their attention to the trenches.

While the artillery duel was being decided, the infantry deployed under good cover at about 1800 yards' range, and worked their way to within 1000 yards of the enemy's position, before they became seriously engaged. Then it was found that the Chinese had disposed their trenches in the form of a wedge, and the inevitable crowding took place, the fire grew heavier, and something, that was almost a check, seemed to have occurred from the slowness of the advance. As a rule Foreign officers have been lavish in their praise of our Indian troops; but one, an officer of high standing, has stigmatised them as being "probably of not much use against European troops." Had he, however, seen the way the 1st Sikhs, 24th Punjab Infantry, and others, on this occasion hung on to their ground, and eventually joined the Americans in the dashing charge they made, he would probably have paused before expressing his opinion in the public press.

The Chinese waited not for the bayonet, but fled to the position in front of the village, whence they again opened a heavy fire. This position, however, was dominated by the one they had evacuated, and the Russian guns, in conjunction with the infantry, soon had completed their rapid flight. Their retreat on this occasion was not so orderly as the first stages of their retirement from Peitsang, but they managed to save part of their artillery, which retired as soon as it became evident that it was outclassed. The enemy's loss was again heavy, amounting to at least 1000 men, of whom nearly 100 perished at the hands of the Indian cavalry who followed in pursuit. Six guns were captured, besides standards, rifles, and more stores.

The Allies' loss amounted to 170, nearly all of whom were British and Americans, truly a slight cost to pay for a victory which finally demoralised the Chinese, who never again plucked up heart to offer another pitched battle. This was almost entirely due to the untiring energy of the Japanese, Indian, and Russian cavalry, who from this day kept in constant touch with their rearguard. The remainder of the 7th August was spent in resting men and horses, some of the Naval Brigade taking advantage of the opportunity to search for all the gear which had been abandoned by Admiral Seymour. The exact spot where all the clothes, etc. had been buried was found, but everything had been dug up, and no traces of the last European visit were visible, with the exception of the burnt and ruined trains, which had been left at the exact spot at which they were abandoned.

Doubtless some portly *mandarin* is still, (1905), wearing the admiral's full-dress clothes, and his children, perchance, appear on swell occasions in the Sunday-go-to-meeting garb of British midshipmen. But even so, it is doubtful if the old gentleman has got much the best of the bargain, for it is at least as certain that some of such midshipmen's female relations are wearing Mrs Mandarin's best sables! After this conspicuous victory it was decided to march again on the 8th, but in such a wretched condition was the French transport and commissariat, that the French had to be left behind to reorganise them.

This delay deprived them of the honour of sharing in the final attack on the outside walls of Pekin, though, as will be seen, they took part in the operations in the city itself. The force was now cut down to Japanese, British, Russians, and Americans, and for some inexplicable reason the order of marching decided on was arranged so that the British marched last, which was rather a serious matter, inasmuch as it meant marching in the heat of the day, and the heat of those days was considerably more than uncomfortably hot. To hazard a guess, it may be presumed that the intense jealousy which prevailed between the Russians on one side, and the British and Japanese on the other, was sufficient to account for it.

Indeed, matters at one time became so bad that it appeared as if each nation would have to act independently in the rush for Pekin. Foreseeing a *fiasco* if this happened, General Gaselee is reputed to have said that the British would march last rather than endanger the success of the whole expedition. This is of course only a rumour, but there is a saying in the navy, "*If you want to know, go to the ship's cook*"; and as there is some truth occasionally in camp rumours, this one is given for what it is worth. The forward march was resumed at 7 a.m. on the

8th, Tsi-Tsun being the next halting place.

The day passed without any fighting, but was the hottest and most uncomfortable of the many hot and uncomfortable ones which were endured during the whole period which the Allies took to reach Pekin. Nearly every one suffered severely, even the Indian troops dropping out of the ranks with alarming frequency. The marines too suffered terribly, and the only men who escaped the effects of the sun to any great extent were the Japanese and Russians, all of whom displayed the greatest endurance. It was thought that some opposition might be encountered at Tsi-Tsun, which was not reached till 6.30 p.m., but not a shot was fired, and the troops camped with the knowledge that the enemy were entrenched near Ho-si-wa, 7 miles further on.

With a possible action in view, the naval guns were ordered to march at 3.30 to take up a position 5 miles higher up the river, and this was accordingly done after very hard work over an unknown country, in the darkness; but when the main body arrived at half-past eight, they were disgusted to find that their efforts had been fruitless, as the Chinese had struck their camp, and evacuated their position, during the night. They were, however, quickly pursued, and a small affair ensued, but all attempts on the part of the Allies to force a general action proved unavailing. An interesting feature of the march was a small cavalry action between the Indian cavalry and the famous Tartars' cavalry. While the matter lasted, the fighting was very spirited, but it ended disastrously for the Tartars, who, outmanoeuvred, over-ridden, and eventually unnerved, fled from the field having suffered heavily. At 4.30 p.m. Ho-si-wa was occupied by the Japanese, after some further trifling resistance.

The town had been entirely sacked by the Chinese soldiery, who had lately made a practice of devastating all towns and villages through which they passed, and who had on this and other occasions caused a very great loss to their own countrymen. Had the force arrived at Ho-si-wa three hours later, the advance would have been seriously retarded, for it was discovered that the banks of the river had been tampered with to such an extent that another hour or two's work would have sufficed to pierce them, in which case the water level would undoubtedly have sunk about two feet, thus necessitating the future transportation of stores by land—a task by no means to be lightly undertaken, with the limited means at hand.

The Chinese were extremely fond of this mode of harassing the advance, and one of these occasions gave rise to a very plucky action on the part of a midshipman with the Naval Brigade. Some lock gates had been forced open against the current, and had been held open by large hawsers and strong stakes which had been driven into the mud; broken glass, bricks, and other rubbish were also requisitioned to back up the stakes. It can be thus seen that it would be a very dangerous task to dive and clear away the various impediments at the bottom of the river, for so great would be the rush of water that in all probability the hawsers would carry away and nip anyone who attempted it. However, the river was wasting itself into a canal, and over the surrounding country, and the water was getting lower and lower, so a midshipman volunteered to close the gates, which he only succeeded in doing after two or three hours' constant diving into 9 feet of muddy water!

A move towards the next town, by name Matao, was made by the Japanese on the 10th, and everything pointed to a stand being made at this place. The naval guns were placed in *junks*, and also started in the early morning, the rest of the force marching at 4 p.m. The difference in the time of starting is accounted for by the fact that by river the distance to Matao is 30 miles, whereas by land it is only 8 miles. But such is the nature of the country, that it was considered preferable to take the longer route, rather than perform the herculean labour necessary to get the guns on their heavy field carriages overland. Had an action, in which they might have been needed, been imminent, the guns would have got there somehow or other, but in this case nothing of the sort was expected, and the matter resolved itself into one of expediency.

At Matao there was practically no stop, and the force pushed on a few miles further to Shan-Matao, being quite unmolested on the march. Here they passed a quiet night, and started at 3.30 a.m. on the 11th, with the intention of occupying Tung-Chow. It was not anticipated that any serious opposition would be met with on the march, but Tung-Chow was a town where there were valuable food -stuffs and other supplies, so that it appeared to be probable that the Chinese might make some attempt at defending it. A few miles before Tung-Chow was reached the cavalry, who were some distance ahead of the infantry, came under a hot fire from a village near the road. The remainder of the troops coming up had no difficulty in turning the enemy out, who were found to be the rear-guard of the main army, and who fled towards Tung-Chow.

The villagers, of whom the great majority were Mahommedans, were loud in their professions of friendliness to the Europeans, and it is quite probable that their display of sentiment was genuine, for not only had the Chinese troops committed all sorts of excesses during their short stay, but the memory of the ruthless severity with which the Mahommedan rebellion of a few years ago was suppressed, doubtless still lingered with them. The Japanese, with extraordinary energy, pushed on without even waiting for a midday meal, and pursued the Chinese until within shell fire of the walls of Tung-Chow. They then opened fire from several batteries, and gave the enemy no rest for an hour and a half, when, eliciting no reply, they waited for the rest of the army, who arrived late in the afternoon. Soon after their arrival, the Chinese commenced a totally ineffective fusillade, which they kept up until dark, when everything became quiet.

About one o'clock on the morning of the 12th, the Allies moved forward to the attack, and by three o'clock the Japanese sappers had blown up the south gate. An hour later, the whole force marched into the town, not having had a shot fired at them since nine o'clock. The previous evening's firing had evidently been a blind, for the enemy had fled towards Pekin before the attack commenced. The 12th was spent in rest, and, as was only to be expected, when the troops found themselves with nothing to do in a captured town, a little looting was done.

It took, however, the mildest form, because it was impossible to carry anything more than articles of absolute necessity, or valuables of the lightest description, and, as most of these articles had already been stolen by the Chinese soldiers, there was nothing much left to take. A great part of the morning was taken up by transferring all the stores, which had come up by water, to various kinds of vehicles, for it was no longer possible to rely on the river as a means of transport. On the night of the 12th, a reconnaissance was made towards Pekin by a battalion of infantry and most of the cavalry, who found that all the enemy had retired within the gates, and that the country to the capital was clear; so it was decided to move on without delay.

The final march commenced the morning of the 13th, and by the afternoon the whole army was drawn up within 3 miles of the city walls. An amusing incident occurred on this day:—

It appears that half a company of the Royal Welsh Fusiliers had lost their bearings the night before, and after some wandering about, had arrived in sight of Pekin itself. Being somewhat weary, they calmly bivouacked and waited for the army, by whom they were found safe and undisturbed some hours afterwards. Now at last had arrived the night before the army's great effort. It found 12,000 tired and thirsty men outside Pekin, not one of whom but felt confident that his next bivouac would be inside the walls. How they and their generals managed to assure this is worthy of another chapter.

CHAPTER 12

Capture of Pekin and Relief of Legations

The Allied generals met for the last time on the afternoon of the 13th to make their final dispositions. It was agreed that the Russians should take the right, the Japanese the centre, and the British and Americans the left. This arrangement came as a surprise to the British, for knowing the intense eagerness of the Russians to be the first into the city, it was supposed that they would have chosen the weakest spot in the defences for their point of attack, whereas it was generally considered that the position they had taken up would certainly bring them in front of the most severe opposition. It was suggested in some quarters that they had argued that behind the strongest walls would be the smaller force, and *vice versa*, so that they might hope to overpower the enemy first, and then force an entrance, whilst the rest of the force would be unable to do either one or the other.

We shall see how they fared. In the evening each force sent out reconnoitring parties towards the walls, that of the Russians being exceptionally large, and including guns. These (the Russians) pushed forward so far without being discovered, that what was intended for a reconnaissance, at length became an attack of an unusually gallant and daring character. After a brisk bombardment at short range, the Tung-Pien gate was forced, and the comparatively smaller body of Russians found themselves the first troops to enter the Chinese city. Their position was by no means secure,—in fact, unless supported at daylight they would be compelled to retire with the loss of their guns, but it was determined to maintain their foothold till the morning, when it was hoped that the main body would arrive.

Daylight came, and with it a tremendous fusillade from the enemy which caused many casualties, but the Russian commander hung on with splendid tenacity, and finally welcomed large American reinforcements. During this important episode, the Chinese made a sortie in some force from their centre, which was beaten back by the Japanese, who, disturbed at their bivouac, decided to push straight on to the walls.

At Pekin, as elsewhere, the little "Japs" managed to get into the thick of whatever fighting happened to be going on, and during the day they were heavily engaged along their whole front. Their persistence did not have its reward until 8 p.m., when their Sappers blew up two gates, and thus they won their way in. Thanks to the precipitancy of the Russian right, the British entered the Shan-huo gate almost unopposed. The Chinese had mistaken the Russian advance guard for the main attack, and had practically deserted their right to cope with it. The British took immediate advantage of this, and forced their way right through to the Tartar walls. Heavy fighting was here expected, but no Chinese troops were in the vicinity, and a signal was got through to General Gaselee to march up the Sluice—a waterway with an aperture through the walls—which was done.

Their advance was unimpeded except by snipers, and at about 2 p.m. a handful of 1st Sikhs and 7th Rajputs broke their way through the rotten Water-gate, and rushed to the Legations, which were but a few hundred yards away. Great as was the excitement then, it became even greater when General Gaselee, his staff (among whom was a naval officer), and men from the 24th Punjaub Infantry, 1st Sikhs, and Bengal Lancers, rode up and greeted the Legation folk whom they had done so much to relieve.

The Legations had been reached, but it must not be supposed that nothing remained to be done. The Chinese were still resisting the entry of the other forces, and had as yet shown no intention of leaving the British and Americans in undisturbed possession of the various gates, portions of the various walls, and other defences which they had occupied. Before, however, relating how the complete occupation of this wonderful four-in-one city came about, there are some impressions to be placed on record, about the looks and feelings of relievers and relieved in the Legations. Naturally enough the first wave of enthusiasm was unreserved—people wept for joy, laughed for the same reason, members of the relieving force were kissed and petted—in fact exactly the same thing happened as always has, and always will happen, at the successful termination of an historical siege.

As usual, too, the relievers were astonished at the clean, almost immaculate appearance of many of the women and several of the men. The contrast was certainly extraordinary; on the one hand a gathering of people who looked at first sight as if they had been picnicking, instead of having borne parts in a long and dangerous siege. On the other a body of men ragged, dirty, and unshorn, who by their appearance could not possibly have been doing anything else for the last ten days but march and fight. It was not until one looked closer that it was possible to realise that these comparatively spotless men and women were tired and worn. and that their white faces and wan looks proved that they had been through as much and more than their ragged but healthy-looking relievers, whose worst enemy had been the sun, and who perhaps could have marched the same distance and fought the same battles straight over again.

There were not many among the besieged who could have stood the strain of the siege over again and lived! Their appearance gave rise to ridiculous, fictitious, and wicked suggestions. One often heard it questioned whether they had such a bad time after all, or, as one man put it,—"Plenty to drink, enough to eat, lots of games, and some first-class shooting! Where's the hardship? In fact, what more does one possibly want?" Other people go to the opposite extreme, and thank Providence that a general massacre did not come off. The only explanation that suggests itself is this. The empress doubtless aimed at the death of the Europeans in the capital, including of course the ministers; but she also knew that, were it proved that she or her troops had had a direct hand in the matter, the revenge that would be taken by the powers would be so awful that the game was not worth the candle.

How then was the matter to be accomplished? Well, she had already pleaded incapability to keep the Boxers in hand, therefore, if they could burn or destroy the Legations and their occupants, she would help them at a distance with her troops and their rifles and artillery. Then it could not be said that her soldiers had actually slain the ministers—in fact she could prove that it was by her orders that eggs and vegetables were taken to them, almost nightly, for a fortnight. It may be said that Imperial troops did actually attempt to storm the defences. Granted: but in such a way that whilst any loss on the part of the defence constituted a great weakness, and therefore, by making these attacks they made the task of the Boxers easier and easier, they did not attempt to push their effort right home; or, from what I have been told by one of the officers engaged in the defence, they must have inevitably succeeded. Why then did the Boxers not succeed? Because there are limits to human endurance: a bullet in the right place is one of them. In other words, because a badly organised and badly armed mob can never hope to close with a highly disciplined, steady, and well-armed body of men a tenth of their own size.

Before an hour had elapsed after the Legations had been reached by the British, it became necessary to dislodge a large number of snipers who had taken up an advantageous position in the Monjol market. This was effected by a bayonet charge by the 1st Sikhs, who suffered but slightly during the operation. Other positions were captured and occupied, and by nightfall the Chinese and Tartar cities were almost entirely in the hands of the Allies. There now remained the Imperial and Forbidden cities to be cleared, and the Peh-tang Cathedral to be relieved.

The next day, the 15th, was a day of hard fighting, hideous mistakes, and the beginning of an era of suspicion and jealousy even more marked than had been the case during the march. Some of the hardest fighting was accomplished by the Americans, who advanced from their overnight position at the Chien-men gate, straight along the approaches to the Forbidden City. This move gave rise to several errors, and much jealousy. Among the former might be mentioned the French firing on the advancing Americans with artillery, and causing several casualties. General Chaffee himself rode back to expostulate, but the combined facts that the French had done nothing during the advance, that they had arrived late, and were also intensely anxious to have a hand in the capture of the forbidden city, had impressed themselves so deeply in the mind of the French general, that for some time he refused to understand the niceties of the situation, and to the protestations of the American general, merely answered, "For the honour of France was not to be served by occasioning the death of his Allies," and desisted from further firing.

The Russians also betrayed their jealousy by endeavouring to share some of the American glory by jointly occupying some of their positions; but General Chaffee would have none of it, and occupied the whole of the approaches to the palace from the Chien-men. In consequence of this move on his part, a conference was held, at which it was decided to delay any entrance into the Forbidden City until all Nations could enter it together. It must be noticed that no such stipulation was in sway when General Chaffee and his men fought their way right up to the very gates; and this officer has been held up to the severest censure for drawing his men off at the critical moment, after heavy loss attendant on constant fighting! Rather should all praise be given him for his forbearance, for doubtless such a prize would have led to endless complications, which were eventually averted by the idea of marching through the city together, and then evacuating it for good, leaving it in the hands of the eunuchs and other palace attendants who were still inside. Other clearing was being carried out by the Russians and Japanese in the north and east, and the British to the south; but the most important work done during the day was the relief of the converts and the others in the Peh-tang Cathedral.

When a true history of that siege comes to be written it will prove even more wonderful than the siege of the Legations. Besieged at the same time as the Legations, the inmates of this once beautiful Cathedral consisted of over 3000 non-combatants, protected by a garrison of 40 marines and 3 officers. Of the latter, 30 men and 2 officers were French, the remainder Italian; their total rifles numbered just under fifty, and their supply of ammunition was very small. Among the 3000 non-combatants were 6 priests, the others being Chinese converts, and the whole being under the direction of Père Favier, a French Roman Catholic bishop, who behaved with the utmost courage and devotion throughout. At the first alarm, this brave man armed as many of his converts as were willing, with home-made spears and other hand-to-hand weapons, which, though they were of no avail against firearms, served to deal with any Boxer rush, which was all that was at first anticipated.

However, as we know, the Imperial troops joined hands with the rabble, and, on June 19th, a gun was brought to bear on the main gate, which it duly blew off its hinges, but such an effective fire was maintained by the handful of marines, that the Chinese abandoned their gun and left it in the open some 200 yards away. A sortie was promptly made, and, with a small casualty list, the weapon and some ammunition were dragged back in triumph. Sorties were, after this success, of constant occurrence, and it was rarely that arms or other warlike material of the greatest value was not found and brought back. For days the garrison were subjected to a hot rifle and artillery fire, then came war rockets and hand grenades, and at last the enemy started mines.

One of these exploded with horrible effect; and another one, the same day, also blew up several houses in its vicinity. The defenders took to countermining, and discovered, and destroyed, several unfinished mines, with such success that it was hoped that this new and more terrible danger was finished with; but in the middle of July, a third explosion took place, which caused the deaths of nearly a hundred people, besides doing further enormous structural damage. So things went on; the French commanding-officer being slain, and many other casualties taking place, until it would seem that human endurance must reach its limit. But no, not a murmur of disloyalty, not a grumble, although the food supply had been cut down, until on August 8th it had almost reached its end, and the miserable ration of two ounces *per diem* was all that remained.

On August 15th, it was realised that relief was near, for the furious cannonading could be heard, and the Chinese were seen to be running hither and thither, in an unusual and alarmed manner; but would it be in time? One day's provisions were left: two ounces of rice remained! It is impossible to state the feelings of those people when the Japanese, closely followed by the French and the British marines, arrived, and they realised that it was all over. It is perhaps just possible to imagine their state of mind, but it would be folly for any one who did not participate in the siege, to attempt to set it down. It will seem almost incredible that no attempt was made by the French to relieve their fellow countrymen on the 14th; when first an entrance had been effected, but such indeed was the case, and so for twenty more weary hours had the half-starved garrison to wait, and hope, and fight.

On the morning of the 15th, General Frey seems to have awoke to his responsibilities, and he asked for assistance, which was forthcoming from the Russians and British. The force reached the cathedral without encountering any serious opposition, at which much surprise was felt, until it was discovered that the ubiquitous Japanese had already raised the siege. In point of fact, a Japanese officer and one man had already entered the defences, but the French may claim the actual honour, shorn of much of its value as it certainly was, of being the first body of troops into the precincts of the cathedral. Then was enacted one of the many dark scenes staged by this civilising army, and especially by the troops of what we are asked to believe is the gayest, politest, and most chivalrous of the so-called civilised nations.

During the movements of the various troops a body of Chinese, some 200 strong, had been driven up a blind alley from which there was no escape. Here they were discovered by the French, and slain everyone,—not by the French alone but by the so-called Christian Chinese converts, who, though so weak that they could hardly crawl, were still possessed of the eminently Christian idea of killing one of their erstwhile tormentors in cold blood. The fighting was over. As for the looting, it was Tientsin over again, only on a larger scale, with more murder, outrage, and rape than had been dreamt of at the latter place. The same degrading scenes were once more everywhere visible, and Pekin was full of men pillaging in every direction. The same excuses as before were deemed to be good enough. The other powers were all eagerly helping themselves to the ownerless valuables, and so good intentions seem to have vanished, and with the exception that our men did not behave like Vandals, they looted like the rest.

In fairness to the English-speaking races, and to the Japanese, it must be said that while they contented themselves with taking unclaimed property, the charges of brutal murder, the ravishing of women, and wanton destruction, were only too often proved against the soldiery of Russia and France. Indeed it may be said that the bestiality displayed by some of the troops of these two powers, beggars description. Excuses, or perhaps explanations would be a better term, can be found for the troops as a whole: the infamous cruelties invariably practised by the Chinese themselves, and the effect such practices exercise on the temper of an army; the confusion existing among the different nationalities, and the infectious example set by the worst of them; and finally the violent reaction and moral breakdown of even civilised peoples, after a long period of intense strain. It is satisfactory to know that even writers with a strong Anglophobe tendency clear our men of the graver charges, and personally, I have over and over again heard the news of such deeds as recounted above, received with the most unqualified expressions of disgust by the men of the Naval Brigade.

In addition to this indiscriminate looting, the various Powers settled down to a little policy of "*Grab who can grab*,"—a game played with much success by the Russians and Japanese, who each secured valuable prizes. All this sort of thing, however, had to end, and the city was divided up into spheres, in each of which one Nation ruled supreme. Proclamations were issued for the purpose of reassuring those of the inhabitants who still remained; and in four or five days' time everything was working more or less smoothly once more. But what of the prime mover in this extraordinary scene? What of the empress and the court? They had escaped by a mere matter of a few hours, and had fled westward to no one knew where, with a huge following of troops and servants. One more act—a farce this time, after so much tragedy,—and we may leave Pekin for good, for the navy had nearly finished their part, and were about to return to their ships.

For a fortnight after all fighting had ceased, the "Forbidden City" bogie continued to worry the various ministers and commanding officers. In 1860 the forbidden city had been spared, and in consequence the Chinese to this day laugh at the idea of any foreign troops ever having entered the gates of Pekin at all. This time it was hoped that at any rate the palace would be burnt to the ground; but to this there were grave objections and powerful objectors. Should this step be taken, it was more than probable that all hopes of getting the empress and her court back to Pekin would prove futile, in which case there would have been no one to treat with, no one with any power to assume authority, which in turn would have meant endless confusion if it had not actually rendered it necessary to pursue the empress over nearly the half of Asia.

It was eventually decided that, pending the arrival of Field Marshal Von Waldersee, the only thing that should be done was to order a military procession, which should move through the city from end to end. This gave rise to a question as to the respective numbers to be engaged, and also to the more important one, as to who was to have the honour of leading the others through the almost sacred precincts. The first was easily dealt with, and it was soon agreed that ten *per cent*, of the total force of each nation present would suffice to show the various flags, and would also be a very fair division of numbers. The other point was more difficult, Japan claiming the honour by reason of her superiority in numbers on the spot, and also because she was generally allowed to have done the most during the relief expedition.

Russia, on the contrary, said that the campaign must be taken as a whole, and that everything being considered, she had the prior claim. It must have caused much heartburning, but eventually Japan acquiesced in this, and the numbers and order of the troops which took part were roughly as follows: Russian 800, Japanese 800, British 400, American 400, French 200, German 200, Austrian 100, and Italian 100, which may be said to have been a very fair division of honour. It may be interesting to give all the important actions during the campaign, and to express from a British point of view the various claims to precedence.

To begin with the Taku forts, it must be allowed that the order of the powers engaged would read: 1st British, 2nd German, 3rd Japanese and Russian. The relief of Tientsin: 1st Russian, 2nd British,

3rd German and American. The first siege of Tientsin: 1st Russian, 2nd British. Admiral Seymour's column: 1st British, 2nd German, 3rd American. Relief of Seymour: 1st Russian, 2nd British. Capture of Pei-Yang arsenal: 1st British, 2nd Russian. Second siege of Tientsin: 1st Japanese, 2nd British (because of her guns), 3rd Russian. Capture of Native City: 1st Japanese, 2nd British and Russian, 3rd German and American. Relief of Pekin: 1st Japanese, 2nd British and American, 3rd Russian. So that, out of nine important military events, allowing for the bracketing of two Powers in some cases, the British gain 3 firsts and 6 seconds; the Russians 3 firsts, 2 seconds, 3 thirds; the Japanese 3 firsts, 1 third; the American 1 second and 3 thirds; and the Germans 2 seconds and 2 thirds.

From this it will appear as though the British were entitled to a voice in the matter of priority, but all the actions mentioned were not of equal importance, and to the Russians and Japanese belong the greatest credit for their share in the whole campaign. On the morning of the 26th, the 250 or so inmates of the Forbidden City surrendered to the Japanese, and on the morning of the 28th, the great ceremony was to take place. At about 8 a.m. the Russian general, General Linev-itch, rode along the British line and passed a few complimentary re-marks about the conduct and bearing of the troops, and immediately after this the 12th Battery of Field Artillery fired a salute as the Tien-an-Men was swung open.

General Linevitch was the first to enter the Imperial City at the head of his contingent, and the rest of the Allies followed in the order agreed upon. Half a mile was passed before the Wu-Men was reached, and once its threshold had been crossed, the Forbidden City had been defiled by the presence of barbarians. Of the actual procession there is not much to tell. As a spectacle it was a failure. Bronzed men, in war and travel-stained uniforms, constitute a very different effect to any of the processions we are in the habit of viewing from 10-guinea stands at home.

The Russians were determined to create an impression, and mounted large guards at the gates both of ingress and egress; from this point of vantage they behaved like the "gods" at a theatre when there happens to be a show of foreign flags. Of course the French were received with immense enthusiasm, such cheering greeting their ap-pearance that all the half-hearted cheers accorded to the other nations sounded almost like an insult. The ceremony passed off quietly, the last to leave being the ministers and generals, and once more the Forbidden City resumed its normal condition. Europe, America, and Japan had taken their moral revenge—it had been a curious one.

CHAPTER 13

Story of the Siege of the Legations

This short but historical siege may be said to have commenced on June 10th, the day on which Prince Tuan was appointed to the Yamen. From the first this high official had shown marked Boxer tendencies, and his first actions were by no means reassuring to the ministers. The usual calls, demanded by etiquette, were left unpaid, and to the end of the siege he remained unknown to the foreign representatives. Between the afternoon of the 10th and the night of the 14th the situation grew rapidly worse, the Summer Legation was burnt, the Japanese secretary was brutally murdered, and the serious news filtered through to Sir Claude Macdonald that the Burg-li-Yamen had decided to attack Admiral Seymour's relief expedition with the Imperial forces.

Then the first military move came from the enemy, who made several half-hearted attacks on the Legation pickets, all of which, however, were beaten off. Several decrees were then issued, all affecting anger at the anarchy which now reigned supreme, and directing the military to take steps to ensure the safety of the persons of the ministers and their families. This was done by posting troops round the Legations, who, being in entire sympathy with the mob, caused unnecessary friction, and added to, rather than detracted from, the difficulty of the situation. A small affray took place between some Chinese and Germans ending in favour of the latter; and at other points there seemed to be a likelihood of the same thing happening; but nothing more occurred till the 19th. In the meantime several peace-members of the government called and discussed the situation with our minister, apologising for what had already happened, and promising to do their best to check the anti-foreign movement.

On the 19th, however, the Yamen notified all the Legations that they considered the attitude taken up by the Powers about the Taku Forts constituted an act of war, and demanded that the Legations should leave for Tientsin within twenty-four hours. An answer was immediately dispatched protesting the inability of the ministers to leave at such short notice, and requesting an interview on the morning of the 20th. To this the Chinese vouchsafed no reply, and after a discussion lasting some minutes, the German Minister, Baron Von Ketteler, disagreeing with his colleagues, decided to make his way to the Yamen accompanied by his secretary. On his way, as every one knows, he was shot dead by a Chinese soldier in full uniform, and the secretary was severely wounded.

Shortly after this atrocity, a reply from the Yamen was received, in which no mention was made of the minister's death, and in which was expressed the regret of the Yamen that it was not considered safe for the Ministerial body to go to an interview, and concerning the short notice to leave, that it was now impracticable. At 4 p.m., in spite of the assurances of the government, the troops opened fire, and the first serious fighting of the nine weeks' siege commenced. During the troublous times just recorded, barricades were erected at every point where there was any necessity for them, but these had been only of a temporary nature; they were now strengthened considerably, and a pre-concerted plan was carried out by which all outlying pickets were withdrawn, all women and children accommodated in the British Legation, and the area of defence defined and condensed.

The British Legation was crowded with refugees, 900 Europeans living there during the siege, the normal number being only 60. The day was spent in provisioning the place and in making all possible defensive preparations. At this time the strength of the combined guards was 18 officers and 389 men, composed as follows:

	Officers	Men
British,	3	79
American,	3	53
German,	1	51
French,	2	45
Russian,	2	79
Japanese,	1	24
Austrian,	5	30
Italian,	1	28

This force does not include 1 officer and 30 men (French), and 1 officer and 10 men (Italian), who were detached to guard the native Christians in the Peh-tang Cathedral. In addition to these there were 125 irregular volunteers who were armed with any available rifles. The artillery at the disposal of the Allies was one Italian 1-pr. Q.F. with but 120 rounds, while the British, Americans, and Austrians, had one machine gun each. None of the guards had more than 300 rounds per man, so that the resources of the foreigners, from an offensive point of view, were positively paltry.

The first man to fall was the Professor of English at the university. He fell a victim to a very misplaced belief in the Chinese, and was killed by cavalrymen whilst returning from delivering a message to Prince Su.

On the 21st, the work of completing the defences was as vigorously proceeded with as the strenuous endeavours of the enemy to break through them would admit; but on the whole the day was a victory for the enemy, for the Austrian barricade was carried, and the French and Austrians who had been defending it were compelled to retreat to the French Legation. The Kansu troops behaved with a certain fierce gallantry, and, although losing heavily, managed to burn the Austrian and Dutch Legations, the Chinese Bank, and part of the Customs quarter. Prince Ching's men behaved in a friendly manner all day, and on one occasion fired heavily into the Boxers, but Tung-fu-Hsiang's men appeared imbued with a most fanatical hatred of everything foreign. During the day all members of the garrison not actively engaged in the defence, occupied their time by organising various committees, such as the Fortification Committee, Food Supply Committee, etc., etc., all of which eventually were of the greatest assistance, and did wonders towards the safety, not to say comfort, of the defenders.

In the evening the Austrian commander took over supreme military command; but on the morning of the 22nd, a rumour having spread that the American Legation had been abandoned, without taking steps to confirm the information, he ordered all the Legations east of Canal Street to be abandoned. There was a stampede. Italians, Austrians, French, and others all rushed alike to the British Legation, and a position of extreme danger was created. Before it was too late the mistake was rectified, and all the forces were sent back to their posts, which were reoccupied with but little loss. After this Sir Claude Macdonald was asked by the other ministers to take supreme command, which he promptly did.

Before the Italians could reach their post, their Legation was found to be burning furiously. In consequence, it had to be permanently evacuated, and the Italians and Japanese subsequently occupied the Su-Wang-Fu, a fine enclosure of about 14 acres, which afterwards played an important part in the defence, although at first it was, through force of circumstances, but inadequately garrisoned. This latter fact formed at the time one of the greatest dangers to the defence; but the holding of this position was unavoidable, as, had it been left unoccupied, the remaining positions would have been seriously endangered.

Another weak spot was the Hanlin library, which, had it been fired, would have caused the greatest danger to the British Legation. Plans were formed to destroy it, but explosives were lacking, and so an opening was made into it in order that offensive operations might be made against any one using it as a sniping-ground, or in case the enemy should themselves determine to fire it. In spite of all precautions, however, the great library was set on fire the next day, and almost entirely gutted; in fact, the Legation itself was only saved by the extraordinary efforts of the defenders, who even managed to save a few of the extremely valuable works with which the building was stocked.

Further incendiary efforts were made by the enemy all along the line, some of which were partially successful; the Russo-Chinese bank was burnt down, the Russian Legation was set on fire—but the conflagration was promptly extinguished, and the Americans were called upon to repel a determined attempt of a similar kind. The enemy's artillery, too, was very active all day, and did considerable damage to the defences; but in spite of this, at the end of the day, the advantage lay undoubtedly with the Europeans.

The 24th was a day of three desperate sorties. Early in the morning the Chinese occupied a portion of the Tartar wall behind the American Legation, whence they could have fired with great effect into the Germans and Americans who were defending the barricades and buildings at this point. They were, however, driven off and pushed back a considerable distance by a brilliant charge, in which they lost somewhat heavily. Almost at the same time the enemy effected a lodgement in the stables of the British Legation. A bayonet charge was made, and the enemy were routed with really severe loss, and a considerable area of cover was destroyed. In this affair, which had a most salutary effect.

Captain Halliday was severely wounded, one marine was killed, and several other minor casualties took place. The officer mentioned accounted for three of the enemy after receiving his wound, and, refusing all assistance, continued to direct his men to the attack. It is gratifying to remark that he has since received the Victoria Cross as a reward for his gallantry on this occasion.

The third sortie was made by the Japanese colonel, in command of a mixed force, who effectually cleared the Customs buildings, causing the enemy further loss.

During the afternoon a barricade was commenced on the Tartar wall, which was constructed under a heavy fire by Chinese converts, who showed great zeal in then: work, and who lost upwards of eight of their number in carrying out this hazardous operation.

On the next day (25th) the government made some sort of attempt to open up communications with the besieged, but the attempt was thwarted by Tung-fu-Hsiang's men, who fired on the bearers of the decree, which curiously enough stated that the Imperial troops were solely to be employed for the defence of the Legations. The only effect which this peaceful attempt had, was to cause a gradual cessation of fire until about midnight, when once more the noisy faction gained the upper hand, and the Chinese again opened fire, this time from behind more substantial cover than they had before been using.

With the exception of a smart attack on the French Legation in the evening, the 26th was passed quietly, but the next two days more than supplied any want of excitement. First the American Legation needed reinforcements, and then the Japanese needed more men to effectively deal with a strong party who were endeavouring to break into the Fu. And they managed to break in, but most of them were carried out! In the evening the troops egged on the Boxers to the assault; this, like all other Boxer attacks, failed disastrously.

The 28th was a day given up almost entirely to artillery. The enemy bombarded the Hôtel de Pékin and the stable quarters, and endeavoured to breach the north wall by firing into it at 20 yards' range. The fire was most destructive, and ceased only just in time. The reason for this respite was probably only the enormous loss in gunners sustained by the Chinese in this absurdly close-range bombardment.

The 29th was perhaps one of the worst days through which the besieged had passed. It was a day of general attack, which was beaten off with the greatest difficulty, and with a loss of life and ground nearly all round. Two sorties, which went out in the early morning, achieved practically nothing, and the harassing day which followed was brought to a close by a tremendous musketry fire, which continued till midnight.

On July 1st the Germans suffered heavily from a surprise, and the French were actually driven out of their Legation. This left the already hardly-pressed Germans in a most critical position, which was only relieved by the prompt measures taken by the British and American Marines. In the afternoon a very gallant but futile attempt was made to capture a small Krupp gun which had been making things unpleasant for the defenders of the "Fu." Owing to the impossibility of thorough reconnaissance of the ground in front of our positions, unforeseen difficulties presented themselves at every turn, and the attacking party lost rather heavily.

The 2nd was passed in strengthening the defences, and in watching the Chinese build a huge barricade about 50 yards away from our northern position, and other threatening redoubts and structures, all of which were nearer than their predecessors. A great effort became necessary, and it was made on the following morning by a force of all Nationalities. In one furious charge the Allied force swept over the enemy's defences, drove him out, and occupied his whole position, thus giving a welcome relief to the Legations. The total loss, owing to the darkness, was trifling, being only 2 killed and 6 wounded. During the day the British flag was shot down, and to hoist it again was at the time impossible, so the staff was lowered bodily and the flag was nailed to the mast.

Among those who helped to replace the mast, it is interesting to note, were the representatives of three of the Great Powers. The next two or three days passed without anything occurring of very great or immediate importance to the besieged; but a runner was sent out on the 4th, and he was, as it turned out to be, the first successful one. The enemy, too, mounted four old 7-pounders, with which they opened fire from the Imperial City wall. It proved, however, to be very harmless, and the crews lost so heavily from our rifle fire and that of the invaluable Italian gun, that they went right out of fashion after a very small period of activity.

On the 6th took place another disastrous little sortie, in the hope of capturing a piece of artillery, and three of the Japanese bluejackets lost their lives in the attempt. On this day the American flag was shot away, and the Russian ensign also had to be moved to escape a like disaster. A very sad event happened on this day. A Russian Consular student, whose mind had become unhinged consequent on the events of the past fortnight, left the French barricade and ran towards that of the Chinese, where he was shot down. It affords some satisfaction, however, to be able to state that eleven Chinamen were killed while trying to gain possession of his dead body. It was now found that the Italian gun had expended nearly all its ammunition.

This was unfortunate in the extreme, but was to some extent remedied by the armourer belonging to H.M.S. *Orlando* who by utilising the percussion cap of a 45 revolver cartridge, and the powder from some Russian shells, refilled the empty cases, the projectile part of the contrivance being cast from pewter vessels which had been found in the neighbouring houses. And it may be of interest to remark that so perfect were these amateur shells that seventy six were afterwards used without one misfire, and with very fair results as to shooting and effect. It was on this day the Boxers and Imperial troops quarrelled and fought a few skirmishes, much to the hurt of the former.

The 8th was made famous by the discovery of a very ancient old cannon by some Chinese converts whilst employed on fortification work. It was dried out, scraped and cleaned, and eventually got ready for service, despite the fact that its trunnions were missing. Such other disadvantages as the lack of sights, ammunition, sponge, and rammer, etc., were quickly got over, and very shortly it fired its first shot, after at least forty years of subterranean slumber. Naturally the practice was erratic, but it was nevertheless very useful at point-blank ranges.

The Fu was hard pressed in the morning, and a new scheme of garrisoning it was drawn up, to relieve the strain on the Japanese and Italians, who had suffered severely in its defence.

The next three days passed with the usual bombardment and ceaseless rifle fire, the "International" as the new—or rather very old—gun was called playing a giant's part in the awful din, though "*its bark was worse than its bite.*" Under cover of this prolonged row, the enemy pushed forward their barricades, and even went so far as to construct a sandbag battery in the Imperial Carriage Park, This battery was the scene of a plucky little action on the part of Sergeant Preston, R.M.L.I., who noticing that the artillery had planted a flag actually touching our advanced post, made a dash for it, in company with the "International's" gunner, and seized it. A storm of firing broke out at this audacious feat, and the sergeant was wounded by some splinters of stone. He was unable to retain his hold of the coveted object, and fell back stunned, but the American gunner hung on tenaciously, and the succeeding tug of war resulted in the flag and half its staff being captured by the Allies. The French sailors in a very similar manner captured a large silk standard from one of General Ma's regiments.

The 13th, the day of the fall of Tientsin city, with all its accompanying fighting, was perhaps the day of the severest fighting which the hard-pressed inmates of the Legations withstood. As usual the position most ardently assailed was the Fu, where the little garrison of Japanese, Italian, and British were literally shelled out of their position, which they had defended in the most stubborn manner. Once behind the next line of defences, the Allies staved off any further advance on the part of the enemy with comparative ease, but other parts of the line were in dire straits.

In front of the Germans the Chinese left their barricades, and charged into the open with great bravery. They were met, however, with a withering fire, and turned to fly. Whilst they were yet wavering, the Germans received a reinforcement of ten Russians, and the combined party charged with the bayonet. This was too much for the enemy, who fled in disorder, leaving one of their standards and many dead.

The attack on the French position was more deadly and more successful. In the early forenoon two muffled crashes were heard in the direction of the minister's house, and it speedily became known that the house, together with that of the Secretary of Legation, had been entirely destroyed by the well-timed explosion of two mines. This caused the French also to fall back on the next inner line of defence with some loss. It was, however, ascertained that the Chinese sappers blew considerably more of their precious selves to glory than the number of Frenchmen they killed, which was only two.

Notwithstanding this fact, the Chinese seemed very elated at the result of their labours, and taking encouragement from the noise and smoke, attacked a position to the left of the one where they had suffered their reverse at the hands of the Germans and Russians. Here they were met by a strong post of Americans, who were, most inopportunely for the enemy, just changing guard, and who quickly sent them to the rightabout.

On the whole, the day had been disastrous for the defenders, who had lost ground at two points, and whose numbers had been decreased by fourteen (five killed and nine wounded). The Chinese, however, did not get off scatheless, and it is probable that their casualties mounted up to at least 150 from all causes.

The 14th and 15th passed comparatively quietly, after this fierce attack, but the noise of pick and shovel betrayed the enemy's intentions of springing some more mines upon the defenders, and steps were taken to foil this measure by countermining. This work was done by Chinese converts, under the guidance of a volunteer from the I. M. Customs. It was now arranged that the Japanese in the Fu should be relieved for some hours' sleep by our marines, and that the transfer should take place early next morning.

This transfer must not be confounded with the slight alterations in the scheme of the defence of the Fu before mentioned. But this necessary arrangement cost the life of Captain Strouts, R.M.L.I., the commanding officer of the British guard; for whilst returning from posting the relieving sentries, he was fatally wounded in the groin, and died within three hours. This was a very serious loss to the defence, as this officer had been of the greatest service and had repeatedly distinguished himself by his fearless behaviour. His death might be termed very hard luck, as it was on this day that the extraordinary truce began, which lasted for four days. It is rather difficult to assign any good reason for the almost total cessation of hostilities on the part of the Chinese, who indeed appeared to be almost embarrassingly friendly for a day or two; but suffice to say it enabled the garrison to repair their shattered defences and to take further precautions against mines.

For four days there was no firing of any sort, and a kind of intercourse sprang up between the besiegers and besieged. On the 18th a messenger arrived from Tientsin with the news of the fall of the city, and the organisation of a powerful relief column. This, of course, was welcomed by all, although many were disappointed that the force was not already on its way. On the same date the enterprising Japs had started a market for eggs and vegetables, which were very acceptable to the hospitals, women and children, all of whom had suffered severely from the want of fresh and nutritious food. It gradually leaked out that this friendliness was due to the disturbing news from the southeast, and that it would only continue until the authorities had decided which course they were going to pursue in the future. Accordingly, no one was very surprised that the supply of food began to decrease more and more, until on the 24th it had ceased altogether. At this time desultory firing began again at any exposed units or bodies of men, and the keenest look-out was kept on the enemy's movements.

On the 28th July a further disappointment was in store for the Europeans, as a messenger got through from Tientsin with a note to the effect that the main body was not even then under way, and urging the garrison to still farther efforts. The Chinese general commanding, too, suavely suggested an immediate and unconditional surrender, pointing out the utter futility of further resistance. A strong reply only elicited a more insistent letter, which again brought forth a still more indignant answer. On the 29th the Chinese commenced a large and important barricade at the east end of the north bridge, which bridge had up to now been swept by the fire of two of our positions. Notwithstanding a brisk rifle fire, the barricade was completed by midnight, and this necessitated several traverses being made to nullify the effect of the fire from behind it. By the 2nd of August the state of the northern and eastern defences was very satisfactory, and steps were then taken to improve those on the west.

A very important and strong position was gained by a sortie in the shape of some strong buildings forming the eastern side of the Mongol market. In its turn this position became the scene of as desperate assaults as the shell- and bullet-stricken Fu, so long and well defended by the devoted Japs, Italians, and a few British marines, had ever experienced. Chinese sappers could be distinctly heard running mines all over the place, or rather all under the place, but their efforts were spoilt, as much by the supineness and dilatory conduct of the master brain, as by the undaunted preparedness of the besieged. Again a messenger got through, this time with a budget of letters, almost amounting to a mail, stating that the relief column had got as far as Peitsang where they had defeated the Chinese. This news exercised a very beneficial effect on the spirits of the garrison. After these little excitements came a lull till August the 9th, when a furious fire was directed against the Fu, upon which, however, so strenuously had every one worked, it made but small impression.

In the meanwhile, news came in that some Shansi troops had arrived who had registered a vow to take the Legations within five days; we shall see how they fared! With the 10th came another tremendous fusillade against the whole of the defences, and further encouraging messages from Generals Gaselee and Tukushima, this time naming the 14th as the probable day of relief. On the 12th the enemy showed many signs of restlessness, and they again opened with their artillery, which had been almost unheard since the truce. Eventually they pressed forward on all sides with great impetuosity—indeed so impetuous were they that they overturned one of their large barricades. For this absurd rashness they paid very dearly, and among the dead was the brigadier-general of the Shansi column. Poor fellow, he will register no more braggart vows!

That day, a day of serious fighting, ended in the utter repulse of the enemy, who had nowhere gained so much as a foot of ground. The 13th was ushered in by sharp firing, and the day was practically a replica of the one before. Once again did the Shansi braves attempt to storm the defences; once again did they get hurled back with indescribable gallantry; and so the fight waged through the day, and the whole night, until early next morning came a lull, when, "Listen! Yes! no doubt of it. Hurrah! hurrah! hurrah!" the first sounds of firing were heard beyond the walls.

The Chinese heard it and understood; an angry and deafening fire broke out from their barricades for a few minutes, and they were gone, gone to endeavour to stem the advance of outraged civilisation, at this very moment clamouring against their gates. How this failed has been told already, and by 3 p.m. on 14th August the British Legation had welcomed the British general and many of his splendid Indian troops. The troops of other nationalities gradually gained their footing in the city, and thus came to an end a siege unlike anything yet recorded in history.

In such a huge myth as Pekin, it can be gathered that all resistance was not immediately crushed; and it was not till two days later that a body of our marines and French troops effected the rescue of the splendid defenders of the Peh-tang Cathedral who, as has been shown in a previous chapter, were even more hard put to it than their equally gallant *confrères* in the Allied Legations.

Much has been said about the "Fu," but below is a return of the killed and wounded in this position alone:

	Killed.	Wounded
British	2	11
French	1	2
Russians	—	2
Japanese	9	21
Italians	7	11
Chinese (converts)	18	85
Austrians	1	1
	38	138

The total killed during the siege was only sixty-six. It will be seen, therefore, that the reports of the fighting in this spot are not exaggerated.

In conclusion let me add a list of the marine detachments officers' casualty list, which was as follows:

Officers	Arrived	Killed	Wounded
British	3	1	2
Italians	2	—	2
Russians	2	—	—
Japanese	2	1	1
Germans	1	—	—
French	3	2	1
Austrians	4	1	2
Americans	2	—	1
	—	—	—
	19	5	9

CHAPTER 16

A Short Comparison of the Troops

A few notes on the equipment, methods, formations, and arms used by the different contingents seems to be not out of place; and as our friends the enemy had such a lot to do with the campaign, it is merely courteous to treat them first. They must be considered in two quite different classes—the Boxers, and the Regular Army. The former were the cause of the whole trouble, and comprised a large percentage of the total male population of Chibliat at the beginning of the outbreak; but their fanaticism rapidly waned as their power decreased, and by the middle of August they became despised even by the Chinese troops, who had once held them in great dread.

An extraordinary feature about their composition was the large number of immature youths and senile old men who flocked to their banner. Their arms consisted of swords and spears, until towards the close of the Tientsin campaign, when they were largely armed with old rifles: a chance of wasting an exceptional amount of ammunition which was eagerly seized upon by these ignorant peasants, who doubtless succeeded in expending considerably more than the ton of lead which is somewhere named as each man's allowance before he is struck. Thus it proves that as foes they were contemptible.

Without formation, without arms, with leaders as ignorant as the common ruck, all that they could hope to do was to murder the few outlying missionaries that stuck to their missions, and to burn their residences over their dead bodies. Women and children became, once their male protectors had been accounted for, an easy prey to the inhuman murderers, who afterwards gloated over their mangled and unrecognisable corpses. Before bitter experience had taught these ruffians a lesson, they were daring in the extreme, and looked down on the Imperial troops with great disdain; but having been placed in the forefront of the engagement on one or two occasions, and having suffered accordingly, they lost their contempt for death surprisingly quickly, and losing spirit, were seen to real advantage for the last time in their attacks on the Peh-tang Cathedral.

Among other incidents of their earlier share in the campaign must be mentioned their attacks on Seymour's column, in which they displayed wonderful faith in the efficacy of their supposed charms, and a still more wonderful fearlessness. In the matter of dress each one pleased himself, but there was a "rig" which proclaimed a Boxer immediately, and which was affected by those able to get the necessary materials. Made, as nearly all Chinese clothes are, of cotton, with the typical Mancha jacket, and loose baggy trousers caught in at the ankle with strings, their attire was in colour blue with a red sash, red waistbands, and red anklets.

The leaders were distinguishable by the large amount of yellow they wore, as did the Buddhists among them, and a final distinctive mark were their red and black standards. These gaudy flags had various mottoes on them; and on seeing a literal translation of one of them, one is not inclined to believe that *"Live and let live"* chanced to be inscribed on any of the others. The sum total of their achievements from beginning to end amounts to very little, consisting as it did of murdering a hundred or so defenceless Europeans; a thousand certainly, probably thousands, of equally defenceless Chinamen, who had either offended them or refused to join them; and doing thousands of pounds' worth of damage to railway, telegraph, and house property, irrespective of their owner's nationality.

Very different in every respect were the regular troops. These were of the best in China,—in fact the troops of Generals Nieh, Ma, and Tung-fu-hsiang are second only to those of Yuan-shi-kai, the enlightened governor of Shantung, who, as some think luckily for the Europeans, preferred to sit on the gate and watch the trend of events, before taking any decisive and possibly disastrous move. He is a very able and progressive man, who doubtless saw the futility of attempting to cope with the world in arms, and so maintained a most correct attitude throughout.

Many if not most of the troops who confronted the allies were foreign trained, it being an interesting fact that among the first instructors who were employed by the government was a naval gunnery instructor from H.M.S. *Cambridge*, also that among the British force during the attack on the Taku Forts was a gunner who had served the

160

Chinese in the late Chinese-Japanese War. Their tactics and movements were certainly somewhat out of date, and consisted for the most part of parade movements, but several times the "attack" was carried out as laid down in the drill book, with the exception of the "Charge and Cheer," without which, of course, the attack is doomed to failure against an enemy who is always disobliging enough to wait for "close quarters." The efficiency of the various armies was to a great extent impaired by the diversity of their arms, and a great deficiency in knowledge of the simplest strategy.

Another point, and an important one, was the utter want of ability to lead their men which was markedly displayed throughout by their company officers. Their general officers seemed capable of drawing their men up to an engagement skilfully, their guns were well posted, and their defensive positions good almost without exception; yet when the range became close there always appeared to be no one in command of the fighting line; the men acted independently, and what had often promised to be an overwhelming attack gradually fizzled away to a bloody repulse.

The movement of a Chinese army must prove a terrible imposition on the people of the district through which it moves, for it lives entirely on the country, and it is doubtful if military mandarins are more honest in their dealings with inferiors than other officials; which means that the army leaves a track of desolation wherever it goes. For the greater part of the campaign the Imperial troops were well fed, but towards the latter stages of the retreat from the Allies, they appear to have been actually starving, and in two instances government granaries were burst into and robbed by the famished men. Their arms were generally excellent, but the ammunition supply must have been a sore trial to whoever was responsible for it.

I have seen the following types of firearms in use by Chinese troops myself, and doubtless others. Sniders, Springfield, Martinis, Marlin, three kinds of Winchesters, three kinds of Mausers, one Mauser carbine, two kinds of Mannlicher, one Mannlicher carbine, and by the Boxers several kinds of *Jingals*, Sniders, Marlins, and Winchesters. As a matter of fact the arms which were used by far the most were the best Mauser and Mannlicher magazine rifles, and whoever did look after the ammunition supply was an excellent organiser, for the enemy had always a seemingly unlimited amount. On several occasions millions of rounds of small arms ammunition were destroyed at a time; but although at all times extremely wasteful, and often firing all through a pitch dark night, they never ran short up to the end.

It is a much debated point whether the Chinese are good rifle shots. Some undoubtedly are, but taking into consideration that the Europeans were generally the aggressors over open country, and always in great numerical inferiority, it would seem that, as their fire was always exceedingly heavy and sustained, the Allies should have suffered more. And yet, glancing at the statistics of the fighting outside Tientsin, and seeing 775 casualties in one day, nearly all from rifle fire, the fact is brought home to one that the Chinese soldiery were not the contemptible foemen that they were supposed to have been by people ignorant alike of their training and arms. The infantry uniform was usually blue or black in colour, with red and yellow facings.

Instead of showing his regiment and battalion on shoulder straps, like his European *confrere*, the Chinese soldier has a white parchment, circular in shape, sewn on to his chest and back, which at any range under 400 yards makes an ideal bull's-eye; and doubtless this idiotic idea was responsible for the death of a great number of them. In shape their uniform approaches very nearly to the national dress, and is admirably adapted to free movement of the limbs. Their headgear was usually missing, but consists of either the little round Chinese hat, or a species of sun hat white in colour. Their boots were of the Wellington variety, into which their trousers were tucked; they had *papier maché* soles, and either cotton or velvet uppers lined with canvas. These boots were both serviceable and comfortable, but owing to the smallness of a Chinaman's foot, when compared to a European's, it was seldom that any of the Allies were able to replace their worn-out footgear from any captured stock.

Their accoutrements were simple, consisting only of a leather belt, on which were carried their ammunition pouches, the frog for their bayonets, and an entrenching tool, very similar to the Wallace spade used by the British. Some carried their ammunition in woollen bandoliers, but the majority were armed with clip-loading rifles, and so pouches were the usual form of carrier to be met with. Their heavy marching order I am unable to describe, never having seen a soldier, either living or dead, so attired. This is explained by the fact that, like the Allies, their radius of action was limited to a few miles round their position, and there was no need of carrying even food with them for more than twenty-four hours. They carried no water bottle for presumably the same reason.

Finally, the Chinese infantryman of today, (1905), only wants good leading to become a formidable foe. With a little more training in addition, there is every reason to believe that they would become a fighting force worthy to rank with our excellent Indian troops.

A different state of affairs is disclosed on coming to discuss the artillery. Here is a thoroughly well-trained and efficient branch of the army, of whom many of the Allied officers spoke with considerable respect, and who, having excellent weapons, used them with effect in nearly every engagement. Their fortress artillery was of the best, comprising guns of the following sizes and denominations: 6-in. Armstrong Q.F., 6-in. Krupp Q.F., 47-in. Krupp Q.F., 9.4-in. Krupp B.L. (nominally Q.F.), 8.2-in. Krupp Q.F., 5-in. B.L. on Vavasseur mountings, and many other breech and muzzle-loading guns of but little value. Their field guns consisted of 3.8-in. Q.F. Krupp, 17-pr. and 15-pr. batteries, 6-pr., 3-pr., and 1-pr. batteries, all of a modern type, and for the most part turned out by the great German gun factory at Essen.

In addition to these, they had several 1-pr. Maxims (Pom-Poms), and in one arsenal alone a large number of Maxims were found, and taken or destroyed. It is impossible to estimate the numbers of each type above mentioned, but their guns were very numerous, and, as in the case of small arms, the supply was good and in plenty; and when it is added that the officers chose good positions for the guns and handled them well, and the gunners were quick at picking up ranges, and accurate in their fire when the range had been found, it goes without saying that the Allies found them a nuisance, the only mitigation of which lay in their capture or destruction.

Of the cavalry but little was seen. They were somewhat *en evidence* during the relief of Admiral Seymour's expedition, when they shaped but poorly; and on one occasion they gave battle to the Bengal Lancers, who entirely defeated a body of Tartars several times as numerous as themselves. They are armed with good German-made swords and excellent magazine Mannlicher carbines, large stores of each weapon being taken at Hsi-Ku arsenal. They were well-mounted on hardy Tartar ponies, well led, and should be a serviceable body of troops. The Chinese soldier then, may be said to be a fair infantry man, a good gunner, but a poor cavalryman. In each case there is room for much improvement, not so much among the rank and file, as among the company leaders and the "Brain" of the army.

British.—At first sight it may seem unnecessary to touch upon either the equipment or the internal economy of any British Force;

but it is an unpleasant fact that but few Englishmen really know what a bluejacket looks like even on board his ship, and still fewer have any idea of his organisation when "clearing up decks" ashore in the out-of-the-way parts of the world, in which his services as a soldier are more often required than is commonly supposed. Thus the matter becomes of interest; and as the looks and methods of the soldiers, both British and Indian, are more easily read about, and therefore more widely known, it is only proposed to treat of the Naval Brigade and the Chinese regiment, which latter was at the time the growth of little more than a year.

The organisation of a body of seamen working ashore is much as follows: A battleship, on receiving orders to land every available man for service like the one we are dealing with, would probably have the following numbers told off: Marines 80 to 100, four companies of bluejackets consisting of one lieutenant, two midshipmen, with fifty petty officers and men each. Two Maxim guns, crews consisting of two officers and twelve men each; two field-guns, crews consisting of eighteen men and two officers each. In addition to these there would be officer commanding and staff, officer commanding marines and staff, one doctor, two sick-berth attendants with medical necessities, four or five signalmen, buglers, blacksmiths, armourers, carpenters, cook's mate, an officer of the accountant branch, and two or three subordinates, one ship's corporal, and a strong stretcher party of stokers under an engineer officer.

Thus it will be seen that each battleship can with ease land 450 men, and is turned out as a complete unit, the men being under their own officers, and self contained in every detail. A bluejacket's arms are identical with those used by the army, but his accoutrements differ somewhat widely. One of the most important differences is the number of rounds carried, and another one is the method of carrying them. In the one case the bluejacket carries 160 cartridges, and the soldier or marine nominally 70, which latter number, however, is always augmented by stowing other packets of ammunition on the person, in the haversack, etc. In the other case the bluejacket is provided with braces on to which two bandoliers are fastened, one going across the body, the other passing along the belt which carries the haversack, bayonet, water-bottle, and the two ammunition pouches.

These two pouches carry—one 60 rounds, the other 40; the bandoliers 25 each, which with 10 rounds in the magazine of the rifle, total 160. Now the marines have only two pouches, both carried in front on the belt, in each of which are carried 30 rounds. The reason for this smaller supply of ammunition is not quite obvious, unless it be that the army always have an ammunition and baggage train, whereas the navy endeavour to carry as much as possible on their persons. It is a point open to debate as to which equipment is the better, but the bandolier system has great advantages.

The cartridges are more easily got at in a hurry, and men are not apt to lose half their ammunition by leaving their pouches open. This generally occurs when advancing to the attack by rushes, and a serious wastage occurs. The fault of the bandolier seems to be that it smothers the men on a long march, by which is meant that it allows of no air passage inside their jumpers. Another point of difference is the gaiter. The navy wear a stout brown canvas legging, very serviceable and much more comfortable than the stiff black leather one worn by the marines, though not so supporting as the more modern *puttie*.

Our men landed in blue serge uniform, and this is the usual fighting rig; the alternatives being white duck—which is, of course, too conspicuous, and was dyed khaki with Condy's fluid, until some of the real article was forthcoming. The marines for the most part landed in their working rig, and generally fought in their shirt sleeves, the exception being the detachment from the *Terrible*, who wore the khaki they had used whilst fighting in South Africa. Their equipment is so nearly akin to the infantry as to require no description.

Warehouses were used as barracks, and all the routine was carried out in a naval manner as much as possible. There was the fo'c'sle, the quarterdeck, forward and aft, just the same as on board ship, the time was registered by striking bells (in this case empty 4-in. cartridge cases) and all orders were given by the pipe,—in fact it was quite evident that the men had in no wise changed from sailor to soldier, just because they were fighting off their own element. For a hospital the British had the English club, and the way that the many cases were treated by a very short-handed staff, with almost no appliances, was little short of marvellous.

In this respect the British force compared very favourably with all other nations, until the main body of the Japanese Army arrived. When moving out from the defences for any distance, the men always carried forty-eight hours' provisions. These consisted of tinned meat and ship's biscuit, palatable and sustaining; each man carried his water-bottle capable of containing about a quart, and it must be noted that several of the ship's companies were supplied with the obsolete wood pattern, which were not especially satisfactory. The commissariat was run by assistant paymasters, and worked smoothly and efficiently throughout, the only wants being vegetables, fresh provisions, and good water in any quantity. The position of the author makes it not only out of place, but impossible, to criticise the methods, tactics, or strategy of the Naval Brigade; but he may be allowed to express an opinion that in keenness, discipline, pluck, and powers of endurance, they, bluejackets and marines, were second to none.

Good alike in attack and defence, it is probable that the results achieved by their labours were at least as important as those obtained by the representatives of any other power. The role played by them in this campaign was almost entirely that of infantrymen, but of course there were occasions when they used their guns. These consisted of two 4-in. Q.F. naval guns on modified "Scott" mountings, several 12-pr. muzzle loading field-guns, which although a disgrace to the service, were used on several occasions with great effect, several 6-pr. Q.F. (used in trains), Maxims and Nordenfelts. The part of artilleryman too was played with striking success at Taku Forts, and speaking generally, the guns of the brigade may be said to have done work of exceptional merit throughout.

The Wei-Hai-Wei regiment was, it can hardly be gainsaid, a great success. Only eighteen months enlisted, they were sent to a neighbouring province to fight under their new officers, against possibly their own flesh and blood, and the way they did it makes Gordon's praise of the Chinese fighting man easily understandable. A part of them had already been tried a few months before, when there was a small rising at Wei-Hai-Wei, in connection with the delimitation of the frontier line, and on this occasion they showed an extraordinary devotion to their officers, and a pride in their discipline worthy of great praise. A story is told to the effect that on the day following a skirmish with the disturbing element, one of the privates asked for a day's leave to go and bury his father.

On being questioned as to the truth of the matter, he assured the officer that it was correct, saying, "Oh yes, me shootee him yesterday." On the present occasion the desire to go to the front was so keen, that crowds of them used to wait on the shore for a ship to come to take them to Taku, and some of them becoming disappointed, deserted. It is worthy of remark that not one deserter took even a cartridge belonging to the government away with him, and they must have deserted in a state of nudity. Their uniform consists of a neat khaki suit—tunic and knee breeches—a sailor straw hat, blue *putties*, and serviceable boots. The queue is worn coiled up beneath the hat. The men are very big, finely built fellows who carry themselves and their uniform well, so that the *tout ensemble* is smart and workmanlike.

The winter uniform consists of a blue turban, blue serge uniform, shaped as before with a red cummerband, and a warm grey overcoat in addition. Their appearance in this uniform is exceptionally clean and businesslike. For arms each man carries one of the excellent Martini-Metfords, a single loader of the same bore as the Lee-Metford and Lee-Enfield rifles, but having the old Martini triangular (section) bayonet. The service water bottle and other fittings are carried in the same way as the infantry. Their share in the campaign was somewhat small owing to lack of numbers, but whenever called upon, they fought well, marched well, drilled well, and behaved creditably always.

The French forces with whom the Naval Brigade had anything to do consisted for the most part of the *Infanterie de la Marine*, and some Tonquinese troops. Some of the regular line regiments, and some excellent artillery, arrived in time to take a not very glorious share in the relief of Pekin, but as they had no opportunities of working with the naval contingents, it is not proposed to attempt a description of them. The French marines, as they were fallaciously called, were clad in a hideous ill-fitting suit of blue cotton. They wore a white helmet trimmed with blue, likewise hideous, and generally worn with the back side foremost. Their heavy marching order was of the heaviest description, and in common with the uniform already mentioned, went far to create a slovenly and unsoldierlike appearance.

Their arms consisted of the Le-Bel rifle, an 8-shot magazine weapon, differing from the majority of magazine rifles in that the magazine is after the old Winchester type, carrying the cartridges up underneath the barrel, and unsatisfactory, because each round fired must materially alter the balance of the weapon. Their ammunition was carried in side pouches, and they had a serviceable water-bottle. The bayonet was totally unlike any used by the various other troops, and was a most cruel-looking article. About 18 inches long, with a white metal handle, and a good method of attachment, its extraordinary feature lies in the blade. It can be likened to nothing better than a long steel used for sharpening knives, yet it was not so thick, and it had four deep grooves running along it from the base to within an inch of the point. It certainly looked a very deadly weapon, but appears to lack strength.

Also, unlike our sword-bayonet, which seems to be the commonest type in use, it is quite useless for any other purpose but man-killing, as it has no edge.

The hospital and transport arrangements seemed good, and the behaviour of the men, until all danger was over, was all that could be desired. Unfortunately, however, there appeared to be a great diminution of discipline after each engagement, and still more so when affairs at Tientsin had quietened down. The men seemed to lack the much vaunted qualities of the French *piou-piou* to a most lamentable degree, and on the only occasion on which a really hard march was called for, before the dreary advance to Pekin, the men straggled terribly. Their native troops, mostly Annamites, were small, of poor physique, and compared in no way favourably with our strapping Wei-Hai-Wei regiment. They were dressed in a sort of Khaki, and armed with an old single-shot carbine with a long sword bayonet.

Their headgear was a board, from which fell a neck covering of Khaki cloth, and their footgear was usually wanting—by which it is not meant to infer that no boots were provided, but that they preferred to march barefooted. The detachment accompanied the French force as artillery, but seemed to be usually employed at fatigue duties, at which they probably excelled. It is at least likely that they were more useful thus, for the little mountain battery which they occasionally laboriously carried about, was as much use as our battery of 7-prs., manned by the Hong-Kong artillery. Of them it was said by a French officer, "*Ils n'aiment pas être tués.*" Whether he expected anyone to affect great surprise, or whether it was his way of saying that they were a little "cold-footed," may be left to the imagination of the reader.

Russians.—Considering the vast amount of experience the Russians must have gained by their long occupation of, and constant service in, Asiatic territories, it is surprising that their equipment was perhaps the least adapted to the climatic conditions of the country, and their accoutrements the least serviceable, of all the Allied forces. This is the more strange when it is probably true that, with the exception of our own troops, those of Russia do more service, akin to active service, than those of any other country. It also certainly seems to be a rash statement which I have seen made, in view of the actual fact, that, after the Japanese, the Russians stood the very trying march to Pekin the best. If so, it would seem to be a case of superior adaptability rather than natural suitability; but of this let more competent critics judge.

The infantry uniform consists of a white cap, with a nearly vertically straight peak, and would seem to give little or no protection to the head. On the upper part of their body they wear a white smock, taken in at the waist by their cartridge belt, and reaching below their hips. Then a pair of baggy trousers, tucked into a pair of Russia leather boots reaching to the knees. The trousers are either a very dark green or black. The various regiments are distinguished by their shoulder straps, which are of various colours, and on which are marked the number of the regiment. The method employed of carrying cartridges is in one way rather exceptional. There is a bandolier, reaching across the chest, which is simply a series of pockets, into which are thrust loaded clips and loose cartridges, all mixed up anyhow, with no attempt at arrangement.

Two pouches are also carried on the belt, which also contain clips and cartridges. Their rifle is the "Mouzin." It is loaded by the clip system, each clip taking five cartridges, but the men carry only a very limited number of clips, and have therefore to use the one clip over and over again. This of course may not be the regulation idea, but it was commonly, and in fact invariably, resorted to in China. It appears objectionable in that it necessitates loading twice, and moreover should a clip get at all dented, it would become difficult to manipulate. There can be little doubt that the Lee-Metford, with its 10-round magazine, would prove superior in rapidity of its fire in any long engagement at close quarters, where magazine fire was much resorted to. The bayonet is a long triangular one, which was nearly always kept fixed, and it was a very noticeable fact that not more than five men in each company had scabbards, and these, where they existed, were of the flimsiest leather, and without any steel cap to prevent the point from coming through.

Only about ten *per cent*, of the men were provided with water-bottles of a uniform pattern. The rest carried flasks, beer bottles, lemonade bottles, in fact anything that would hold water, suspended from their belts with a piece of string. From this it may be gathered that their equipment was very easily visible, of a very rough description, and certainly neither the most formidable nor the most comfortable of those amongst the Allies. The men themselves are brave and stolid soldiers, excelling at defence rather than attack, in which latter they are extremely slow, losing many men from gunfire while still out of effective rifle range, and yet not appearing anxious to close. A defect in their organisation appeared to be that the regiments were under officered, and that the "non-coms" had not that command over their men which they ought to have, when their commissioned rank is placed *hors de combat*. The Russian bluejackets were dressed in a somewhat similar style to ours, and their arms and accoutrements were identical with those used by the army. To sum them up, it was remarked in Tientsin, with great truth, that the Russian soldier in battle was a splendid man, but afterwards a licentious brute. This, though a very comprehensive accusation, was only too true on many occasions in North China.

Americans.—It is doubtful whether there was a more sensibly clothed or better armed body of troops in China than the Americans. The Marines wore soft brown felt hats, a blue flannel shirt, warm and comfortable, and khaki knickers with dust-coloured leggings. The regulars dispensed with the shirt and wore a khaki tunic instead. Both forces wore brown lace-up boots with exceedingly soft and comfortable uppers. The men carried blankets and ponchos for the bivouac, the latter being merely a waterproof cape with a hole for the head, comfortable, very light, useful, and, if necessary, capable of being folded up and put in one's pocket. The rifles used were the Lee straight pull, and the Krag-Jorgensen, perhaps the worst and the best types of rifle at the front. The first, a rather complicated clip-loading rifle, firing a bullet of such a small bore, and light weight, that it was a hopelessly inadequate stopping weapon: this was only used by a small contingent of Marines straight from the Philippines, who had had no opportunity of being re-armed.

The Krag-Jorgensen, on the other hand, is a .300 bore rifle, with a magazine containing ten shots. The whole mechanism lends itself to simplicity and speed, jambs are infrequent, and structurally the rifle is capable of standing a large amount of wear and tear. With these advantages, in addition to very accurate sighting, the champions of the Krag-Jorgensen may well claim that the American army possess the most formidable rifle in existence. The bayonet is similar to ours, but, whereas, our bayonet is fixed underneath the rifle barrel in the same straight line, the American bayonet is fixed on the side of the barrel, and horizontally to it. Their ammunition was mostly carried in bandoliers round the waist. These are made of woollen material, and are double all the way round.

The water-bottle is of metal, very large and most serviceable. The American cavalry were horsed on very heavily built chargers which were not at all suitable to the country. Their accoutrements differed but little from the infantry. Of course riding-breeches and top boots took the place of knickers and leggings, otherwise the dress was the same. They were armed with carbine and sword, which, according to British ideas, never was an ideal cavalry armament, and is now perhaps less so than ever. The American organisation was undoubtedly good and thorough, but in many cases the personal element spoilt everything. For instance, whilst their hospital corps was better off for stores, instruments, etc., than our own, we had fewer amputations by many, and no cases of gangrene, as against twenty or more which they had, a sad case of which occurred after the severe fighting outside Tientsin City.

Leonard, a lieutenant of marines, was shot below the elbow. The arm was amputated above the elbow, soon after which gangrene set in, making another amputation necessary. Again gangrene supervened, and a further operation was performed. But thanks to a splendid constitution and indomitable pluck, this fine young fellow and gallant officer survived not only the wound, but the drain and strain of the operations it necessitated. Much more might be said and many more incidents told of the American forces, but the brightest page in their annals in China was the famous fighting at Pekin, where both infantry and artillery distinguished themselves, and added a page to the military history of their army of which no American will ever be ashamed.

The Japanese.—As was to be expected, the Mikado's nation took a large part in the Chinese imbroglio (?) Not only did Japan send the largest contingent, but the personnel perhaps excelled more than that of any other nation. There are many reasons why this should have been so, principally because the Japanese have once before engaged in a war with China, whereby the officers and men gained great experience of Chinese methods—a valuable asset totally lacking among many of the other Forces, and an experience which, from the first, ensured suitable organisation and equipment, and which the British Indian troops, and the Russians in a lesser degree, alone could hope to equal. Thus it was that, departmentally at any rate, the young Eastern nation outshone its European *confrères*. There were other reasons which led up to the result that the troops of our new Ally came out of the war with such a monumental prestige.

It must be remembered that officers and men were for the first time engaged shoulder to shoulder with their brothers-in-arms from the West, and this alone was sufficient to put them on their mettle, and to cause such patriots as they are to strain every nerve to uphold the honour of their country. Their transport arrangements were both sufficient and efficient, one point to be noticed being the carrying of large numbers of Japanese *coolies* on board to do all the disembarking, re-embarking, and general fatigue duties inseparable from the moving of an army corps. The men themselves were excellent. Small and compactly built as they were, there was such a little difference in size between them, it was a common joke that the whole Japanese army were outfitted by a ready-made firm who only made one size of clothing. They were armed with an 8-shot Magazine rifle, a weapon something on the lines of a Le-Bel, but differing essentially in many ways.

To begin with, the bore is nearly square, though the bullets are conical, and the bayonet is a small edition of ours, more slightly built and with a somewhat different attachment. The rifle is called the "Murata" after its inventor, who by the bye, was a naval lieutenant. Their uniform consisted of a black tunic, white German cap, white trousers, white spats, and serviceable boots. As far as colour went, it was too visible, and the Japanese authorities have decided henceforth to adopt khaki. Their ammunition is carried in pouches and on the person. Besides his weapons, the infantryman carries a water-bottle and a day's ration always when going out to fight. The men march well, shoot well, are well disciplined, and know no fear of anything; add to this skilful and fearless leaders, and we have worthy rivals to our British infantry. Though small, the Japanese have a decided penchant for close quarters and cold steel—yet another link between our armies.

The cavalry are perhaps the weakest branch of the service, not on account of any human deficiency, but rather because of the small size of the horses. These are not altogether suitable for several reasons, among others that, being entire horses, they are exceptionally savage, and in camp cause great trouble as well as many casualties. Then again, on account of their lack of weight, they are unsuitable for shock tactics. This, however, did not prevent them from carrying out one of the most effective charges in the campaign, nor did it prevent them from rendering scouting services beyond all praise, during the advance on the capital. Their weapons were the sword and carbine. They appeared to be well trained, and with no defects except those already mentioned.

The Japanese artillery are armed with a Q.F. gun, throwing a shell of about 14 lb. weight. They are smart and efficient. The uniform worn by them hardly differs from that worn by the infantry. The hospitals, both base and field, were wonderfully good, prompt and skilful attention being received by all the wounded, who were certainly better off in this respect than those of any other nation. From these few remarks it may be seen that we are allied to a nation with an army strong in numbers, well skilled in war, brave to a fault, and still further allied to our army by many points of close similarity.

It should be mentioned that the behaviour of the Japanese troops was exemplary, and that in this respect they could give points and a beating to nearly all the other troops engaged. Among many equally gallant actions performed by Japanese troops, one stands out pre-eminent. It was the storming and blowing up of the south gate of Tientsin, the deciding move in the most important engagement of the war. In days to come the Japanese will talk of it as we talk of our sappers at the Cashmir gate, Delhi!

The other nations engaged in the campaign were Italy, Austria, and Germany, but although the services of the representatives of the first two named were valuable at a time when every rifle counted, their numbers were too small to admit of an excuse to describe them, and in doing so to spoil more paper. Even Germany hardly shone in the operations, notwithstanding her shriek of vengeance, and the soul-stirring speeches made by the *Kaiser* to his departing troops. They, however, deserve some mention, even were it only because Field Marshal Von Waldersee was the commander-in-chief, recognised by all the Powers concerned. He, with most of the German troops, arrived too late for any serious fighting, but for the rest of the operations he showed the greatest capacity and tact, and did much not only to bring the campaign to a close, but to preserve at any rate the semblance of a peace between the Allies, who, immediately after the fighting was over, began to quarrel amongst themselves.

The *Iltis* too, at Taku forts, wrote a glorious page in the naval history of her empire, which was added to by the devotion and gallantry of the German sailors under Seymour. In conclusion, it may be said that it was Germany's misfortune, not her fault, which forbade her taking a more glorious share in the work of punishing China, against whom she had a more genuine grievance than most of the other Powers.

CHAPTER 15

Return of Naval Brigade, Peh-Tang and Shan-Hai-Kwan

After the events recorded in the twelfth chapter, it became certain that the navy's share of work on shore had been completed. However, the brigade with its guns remained in Pekin for about a week before the order was received to return to shipboard. This was recognised to be inevitable now that the army had come, and, on the whole, the men were ready to welcome the change back to their proper role. The Pekin Brigade embarked on *junks* at Tung-Chow, and after a very uneventful journey, arrived at Tientsin on the 3rd of September. Here they picked up the remainder of the force with the exception of Captain Bayley, R.N. (provost-marshal), and his personal staff, and returned to their ships on the following day, in tugs and lighters. Thus, on the 5th September, the only representatives of the senior service ashore were the Blue Marines, a hundred in number, who were left to garrison the Northwest fort, until the time came for its demolition, and the three officers and two men at Tientsin.

A most satisfactory thing was it to grip one's messmates by the hand again, and receive their congratulations on one's safe return, a feeling marred only by thoughts of the missing, about whom many questions had to be asked and answered. Outside the bar, quite close to the fleet, lay the *Salamis,* on board of which were upwards of 300 men of the New South Wales and Victoria Naval forces. It was hoped that these fine fellows would be in time for the occupation of Pasting-fu, which operation was about to be undertaken by a combined British and French force. Most of them did take part in this movement, but unfortunately, either the policy of "Let's get there first, never mind existing arrangements," or an utter lack of appreciation of combined movement, was responsible for the fact that, when the British force arrived in front of the town, it was but to see tricolours floating at every point.

The place had fallen, with a very slight resistance, and was occupied, because it was the headquarters of the Boxer movement, and the scene of many early atrocities. To the eastward of Taku, distant about seven miles, lay some other powerful forts called Peh-tang. The arrangement which had allowed them to exist during the past three months had been an eminently commonsense one, when it is considered how the Allies were pressed for time and men. It was simply this, "You don't hit me, and you won't get hurt," an arrangement fulfilled to the letter by both sides. It was, therefore, with feelings of surprise that I, having finished some duty which took me to Tientsin, and having a day or two to look round, heard that the French, Russians, Germans, and Austrians had decided to break the agreement, and attack the forts. I went down to Tong-Ku with the French officers, and hoped to be allowed to go with them, but on arrival I found that our two 4-in. Q.F. guns were being brought up to entrain, and that the marines from the fort were to be their escort.

This was much better, and I immediately attached myself to the officer in command of the latter, and we waited impatiently at the station for the guns. To everyone's great disgust, the only available trucks were not large enough to take the improvised field mountings, and the Russian officer in command of the station would not allow them to be broken. This, of course, did away with the necessity of an escort, and much to their disgust, the "Joeys" were marched back to the fort at two in the morning. However, by dint of hard walking, a marine officer and myself managed to see enough of the action to justify a very short account of it.

The Allies attacked from the direction of Taku, and numbered in all about 2600, with a battery of howitzers (Russian) and some French and German artillery. The engagement commenced at about one o'clock in the mornings with occasional shots from the forts; but it was not until daylight that the heavy Howitzer battery replied, and the fight became general. After a somewhat protracted bombardment, a general advance took place, and the force was almost unopposed from this time. Indeed, so slight were the losses of the Allies, that it at one time seemed as if the whole affair was a "put up job," and this supposition was further strengthened by a temporary lull in the proceedings at about eight o'clock. The advance was again continued about 9 a.m., and by 10.30 it appeared as if the forts had been evacuated. Up till now, the attacking forces had been beyond the range of effective rifle fire, but at eleven o'clock, a bridge about 2000 yards away from the nearest fort was demolished, and shortly afterwards the trouble commenced. The small company of Austrian bluejackets was marching along quickly, when a tremendous explosion took place, and the head of the company was literally blown to pieces. A sailor had trodden on a contact mine, and the result was—one officer killed, one wounded; three men killed and twelve wounded, three of whom afterwards expired. This was the first of a series of explosions, several of which took effect, the most notable being that which caused the death of a Russian Engineer officer, who had been indefatigable in his exertions to find and destroy these deadly weapons before they could do any harm; one, more cunningly hidden than the rest, practically blew the poor chap to pieces.

No further opposition being encountered, the two forts were successfully occupied by one o'clock, when it was clearly demonstrated that the Chinese had left some hours since. It is doubtful if the enemy lost more than a dozen men in this ridiculous action, while the loss of the Allies was but slightly larger. It should be mentioned that the British were carefully prevented from taking part in this action by the lack of proper intelligence, and by being thwarted at every turn by the Russians, who only sent word to the Australian brigade when it was too late to leave Tientsin. Curiously enough, but perhaps for the same reasons, neither the Japanese nor Americans participated, but it must be admitted that, but for the use of land mines, the affair was neither very difficult nor particularly exciting.

A more interesting, and, to the British, a much more satisfactory affair, shortly happened at Shan-Hai-Kwan. This place is situated between 150 and 200 miles to the north-eastward of Taku, and is the site of some more very powerful forts. It is also a railway terminus, and once had some slight strategical importance on account of being the place where the Great Wall of China comes down to meet the sea. It possesses no naval value, being an open roadstead, and ice bound during the winter months. It became imperative to take the forts on account of the valuable line of communication afforded by the railway, and because of the possibility of the place becoming a rallying centre for the enemy. The "Whens" and "Hows" were the reason for many conferences between the admirals; and it became evident that, to them, it appeared to be a difficult and risky matter, and one, moreover, likely

H.M.S. "BARFLEUR"

RAILWAY CROSSING GREAT WALL AT SHAN-HAI-KWAN

to entail severe loss on the attacking fleet. This conclusion having been arrived at, the difficulty arose of choosing a leader who would make all the arrangements, and hold himself responsible for the result.

I have heard, but refuse to be responsible for the statement, that both the French and German admirals were asked if they would care for the task, but declined on various grounds, and that then Sir Edward Seymour was requested to deal with it, and at once accepted the responsibility. What credence can be placed in the former part of this I do not know, but the latter part of it is undoubtedly true, and the British commander-in-chief took the work of organisation in hand forthwith.

As far as the arrangements became public, it was believed that Admiral Seymour intended to employ none but armoured ships for the bombardment, and the fleet would probably consist of H.M.S. *Centurion*, *Barfleur*, and either *Aurora* or *Orlando*, the first two being battleships and the others armoured cruisers; *Navarin* and *Sissoi Veliky*, (Russian battleships), two German, one French, *D'Entre Casteaux* one Japanese *Tokiwa* (armoured cruiser), one Austrian battleship, and one Italian armoured cruiser, being a total of, roughly speaking, a dozen heavily armed ships. Before sailing, however, the *Pigmy*, a small gunboat, was sent on ahead, with a political officer on board, who was told to endeavour to parley with the Chinese commanding officer. So the little ship stood right in under the forts and lowered a boat, when to the captain's surprise the Chinese ware seen to be streaming out at the back of the forts, and running up to the hills. He immediately grasped the situation, and sent one officer and seventeen men ashore to garrison the five big forts, and to hold them against all comers.

He then went back to Taku as fast as possible, and told the admiral what had happened. Was there ever such a ridiculous situation? The forts had been taken by that powerful and important ship H.M.S. *Pigmy*, and were at that moment held by the overpowering force of one naval officer and seventeen bluejackets; whilst at Taku were waiting a dozen or so leviathans, with 7000 men at least on board, who as yet were not aware that they had been baulked of their prey by the aforesaid gunboat of considerably under 1000 tons! However, the news had not to be told just yet, and in an hour's time the *Pigmy* was hurrying back for all she was worth, packed with marines to assist the so-called garrison. At last she disappeared over the horizon, and then the secret was let out. Sparks and clouds of smoke were soon issuing from the funnels of the fleet's cruisers, and one by one, as they raised enough steam to move, they got under weigh for Shan-Hai-Kwan to see what had really happened.

What had happened was as equally ridiculous as the rest of the farce, for during the night much tramping was heard around No. 1. Fort, as if an army had come down to retake the place. And, as a matter of fact, this is more or less what the noise represented; for the force turned out to be 4000 Russians, who in their guileless way, had turned up from goodness knows where, to surprise and capture the forts, without a word to any of her very good Allies! "Halt! who goes there?" and the column halted out of sheer surprise.

"Who are you," from the other party. "The officer commanding the British garrison of Shan-Hai-Kwan forts," and so on, till at last the Russian colonel, smelling a rat, asked to go in.

"Very sorry, strictly against my orders, you'd better encamp in the open tonight." Sounds of much discontent from outside, and then, still being dissatisfied about the *bona-fides* of the occupation, the column began to solemnly march round each fort, only to be challenged time after time by the active sentries, who, by dint of hard running, passed and repassed each other, with the effect that the forts appeared to be strongly held. The Russian column, therefore, retired to the railway station, where they encamped until authority arrived to give the forts up to the Allies. This was done, the British laughing heartily for some days to come, at the "capture of the Shan-Hai-Kwan forts."

Now, it may be gathered from the recent half-hearted operations, that the enemy had had more than enough of the struggle, and indeed, from this time to the conclusion of hostilities, the campaign degenerated into the hunting down of robber bands, the destruction of Boxer strongholds, and the almost vain endeavour to prevent actual collision between the Powers. Tientsin seemed to be the chief place for the important affrays, which might have led to more serious consequences had it not been for the prompt measures taken for their repression.

A drunken Russian officer was shot dead by a German patrol, English officers were pulled out of their *Jinrickshaws*, two Russians were shot by an American sentry, a British patrol was attacked by 250 French and Germans, every member of it was hurt, but seven killed and eleven wounded was the bill on the other side. Without American assistance, it is extremely doubtful whether it would have won its way back to barracks. A mad *sepoy* killed a comrade, and then rushed to the Russian barracks, where he killed a warrant officer, and wounded three men. This led to an affray between some of his own comrades, who were chasing him, and the Russians, who imagined that they were being attacked, which only resulted in further loss.

And so on, and so on; with incidents like the Tientsin railway siding, to set the world's Press on the jabber about war. It appears that some dispute arose over the piece of ground in question, which ended in Russia placing double sentries on it. The British immediately did likewise, to prevent any advance from the further side. Matters stood like that, until the Russians put half a company there, when half a company of Indian troops immediately faced them. This was really rather critical, as but four or five yards separated the two bodies, who stood, with loaded rifles and fixed bayonets, eyeing each other with the greatest suspicion.

At this time, the French soldiers off duty used to come up in considerable numbers and make use of the most filthy expressions anent our Indian troops, calling them *coolies*, and worse. This so enraged the men, who throughout the latter part of the campaign had affected to utterly despise the French, that it was evident that white soldiers would have to be employed, and, no others being available, a detachment of Royal Marine Artillery, than whom no finer body of men exists was brought from the forts at Taku. The changing of the guard was effected by night, and when the French arrived next morning, they were much astonished to find themselves faced by a body of men who, even on the colour question, could hardly be called *coolies*. This little incident, together with the efficient police work afterwards carried out by the Australian sailors, completed the work of the Naval Brigade, and except to the offices and men who took part in the operations, the China Campaign means but little.

Not much remains to be said. How the Rising nearly spread to the Yangtse, but was stopped by the powerful Yangtse Viceroys, is common knowledge. A fleet, of course, gathered at Wusung at the first sign of trouble, and a few little things are worth recording. For instance, the Chinese were completing the armament of the powerful Yangtse forts with feverish anxiety, and, on one occasion, they found some difficulty with the mounting of a 15-cm. "Krupp."

A certain officer happening to notice this, took charge of the party with the greatest assurance, and, Hey Presto! down came the whole show, much to every one's disgust. On another occasion two midshipmen managed to crawl into the forts, and had a good look round before they were discovered and ejected. After this, the Chinese threatened to shoot at any football parties near the forts, and the fleet's playground had also to be shifted. Occasionally the Chinese navy used to show up, and it was a funny sight to see a Chinese cruiser passing up the river, with the guns of one of our armoured cruisers laid for her water line as she passed, and following her up until out of range.

An equally funny sight must have been one of our tiny river gunboats lying under the 12-in. guns of the upriver forts, pretending that she was only waiting for the big 'un to start hostilities, before knocking down the whole place. While things were still a little touchy, Chinese New Year arrived, and it was rumoured that on that night the forts would open on the fleets. Every preparation was made, but nothing happened, and eventually the fleets quietly dispersed to their respective spheres to give that much needed leave which all their hardworked crews so thoroughly deserved.

The Naval Brigades had done their work. Who shall say it was not as satisfactory as it was important, or that the British Contingent was found wanting in any way from first to last? The same traits which have made it the envy of the world—the initiative, the daring, the dash—found ample scope in China, and were equally conspicuous there, as they have ever been elsewhere, when duty called for their display, in upholding the glorious traditions of the Senior Service, and of our ever increasing Empire.

www.ingramcontent.com/pod-product-compliance
Lightning Source LLC
Chambersburg PA
CBHW021101090426
42738CB00006B/456